D1142004

SAGE was founded in 1965 by Sara Miller McCune to support the dissemination of usable knowledge by publishing innovative and high-quality research and teaching content. Today, we publish over 900 journals, including those of more than 400 learned societies, more than 800 new books per year, and a growing range of library products including archives, data, case studies, reports, and video. SAGE remains majority-owned by our founder, and after Sara's lifetime will become owned by a charitable trust that secures our continued independence.

Los Angeles | London | New Delhi | Singapore | Washington DC | Melbourne

Why
I Am Not
a Hindu

Why
I Am Not
a Hindu

**A Sudra Critique of Hindutva Philosophy,
Culture and Political Economy**

Kancha Ilaiah Shepherd

Los Angeles I London I New Delhi
Singapore I Washington DC I Melbourne

First published by SAMYA, an imprint of Bhatkal and Sen, 16 Southern Avenue, Kolkata 700026, in 1996; eighth reprint 2003.

The second edition was first published in 2005; reprinted 2007, 2009, 2012, 2016, 2017.

This edition published in 2019 by

SAGE Publications India Pvt Ltd
B1/I-1 Mohan Cooperative Industrial Area
Mathura Road, New Delhi 110 044, India
www.sagepub.in

Samya
16 Southern Avenue
Kolkata 700026
www.stree-samyabooks.com

SAGE Publications Inc
2455 Teller Road
Thousand Oaks, California 91320, USA

SAGE Publications Ltd
1 Oliver's Yard, 55 City Road
London EC1Y 1SP, United Kingdom

SAGE Publications Asia-Pacific Pte Ltd
18 Cross Street #10-10/11/12
China Square Central
Singapore 048423

Published by Vivek Mehra for SAGE Publications India Pvt Ltd, typeset in 10/12 pts Centurion Old by Zaza Eunice, Hosur, Tamil Nadu, India.

Library of Congress Cataloging-in-Publication Data Available

ISBN: 978-93-532-8262-2 (PB)

SAGE Samya Team: Amrita Dutta, Guneet Kaur and Aritra Paul

To my mother,
Kancha Kattamma,
whom we lost in 1967.

Thank you for choosing a SAGE product!
If you have any comment, observation or feedback,
I would like to personally hear from you.

Please write to me at **contactceo@sagepub.in**

Vivek Mehra, Managing Director and CEO, SAGE India.

Bulk Sales

SAGE India offers special discounts
for purchase of books in bulk.
We also make available special imprints
and excerpts from our books on demand.

For orders and enquiries, write to us at

Marketing Department
SAGE Publications India Pvt Ltd
B1/I-1, Mohan Cooperative Industrial Area
Mathura Road, Post Bag 7
New Delhi 110044, India

E-mail us at **marketing@sagepub.in**

Subscribe to our mailing list
Write to **marketing@sagepub.in**

This book is also available as an e-book.

Contents

Preface to the Second Edition

I am pleased that this book, published in 1996 and reprinted eight times, is now in its second edition. I have provided an Afterword that discusses the reactions of the readers and the way the book influenced theoretical discourse in India and abroad. I am particularly proud that the book has served as a manifesto to the cause of the Dalitbahujan's fight for social injustice. Most important, the book has also thrown up an alternative concept—Dalitization—to the brahminic concept Sanskritization. The last chapter of the book was reprinted in *Postcolonialism: Critical Concepts in Literary and Cultural Studies,* edited by Diana Brydon (5 vols, Routledge, 2000), which has meant that the concept has been globally validated.

Hyderabad, June 2005

Preface to the First Edition

This book is an outcome of my constant interaction with the Dalitbahujans in the Dalit and civil rights movements, who kept telling me, in a variety of ways, about their culture, economy and politics. What I have done is to put their ideas down in a systematic way. Apart from my personal experiences all the ideas in this book are picked up from illiterate and semi-literate Dalitbahujans and also from a few formally educated Dalitbahujan organic intellectuals.

On several occasions my upper caste friends—women and men—have discussed the socioeconomic life processes in their castes and families with me. Such discussions were of immense use in building a critique of their culture and economy from the point of view of Dalitbahujan culture and political economy. I thank all those friends.

After I had completed the draft Susie Tharu, Duggirala Vasanta and Manohar Reddy involved themselves fully with it, shaping the book into its final form. In fact they spent so much time on it that it virtually became their adopted child.

All the members of Satyashodhak contributed by participating in our regular '*adda debates*' (the place where villagers gather together to discuss village problems is known as *adda*), sharing my ideas and also criticizing them. Special mention must be made of Dr S. Simhadiri and A. Ramanatham whose critique enriched some chapters. Rama Melkote, Veena Shatruguna, K. Lalita and Paroma Deb made useful suggestions. The suggestions that Lalita offered were of great use in the analysis of Brahmin life-processes, as they have been presented in this book.

My niece Rama and nephew Krishna Kanth typed the first draft and G. Ramalingam of Osmania University keyed it on the computer. R. Srivatsan came to our aid whenever computer technology created knots. In the process Srivatsan, who is a scholar himself, read the manuscript, gave me much-needed encouragement, and offered his valuable comments. My sister-in-law, K. Bharati, brother Kattiah and two younger nephews K. Naresh and M. Surender helped in several ways while I was writing this book. I thank all of them.

A NOTE ABOUT TERMS AND CONCEPTS

I would like to say a word about the terms and concepts that I use in this book. I have not used terms like 'lower castes' or 'Harijans' while referring to the Other Backward Classes (OBCs) and Scheduled Castes (SCs) because the very usage of such terms subordinates the productive castes. Dalitbahujan history has evolved several concepts and terms to refer to the castes that constitute SCs and OBCs.

Mahatma Jyotirao Phule, who perhaps was the first modern thinker to write about all productive castes, had characterized them as 'Sudras and Ati-Sudras'. There are problems in using the same concepts now. At that time there was no clear division between 'Sudra upper castes' (whom I characterize as Neo-Kshatriyas in this book) and the OBCs in general. All those castes that did not fall under the

category of Brahmin, Kshatriya, Vaisyas were called 'Sudras' and all
the so-called untouchables were called 'Ati-Sudras'. This kind of
conceptualization has its own problems. The concept 'Sudra' has been
used by brahminical writers in a derogatory sense. It does not
communicate a feeling of self-respect and political assertion. Phule's
usage, however, is to be preferred to the abusive brahminical terms
like *Chandala, mleccha, raaksha,* and so on; even an anglicized term
like 'untouchable' is equally unacceptable.

Many sociologists used the term 'caste Hindus' to refer to all
castes which are outside the Scheduled Castes. This terminology is
a trap for the OBCs. In their day-to-day lives the OBCs are as
oppressed as are the Scheduled Castes by the 'upper' castes. Yet
the term offers the OBCs inclusion in the 'Hindu' fold—but only as
unequals. I, therefore, reject this terminology outright.

When Ambedkar began to write about these castes, the British
Government of India was using the term 'Depressed Castes' to
denote all working castes. For a long time, Ambedkar used the same
concept to denote all productive castes. After the colonial government
set up a schedule in which reservations were to be provided for the
'untouchable' castes, Ambedkar used the term 'Scheduled Castes'—
of course, to refer only to the so-called untouchable castes. However,
he never developed a similar secular term that could refer to the OBC
castes collectively.

Ambedkar gradually shifted to using 'Dalit', a concept that is
rooted in the Marathi language, to refer to Scheduled Castes. The
word 'Dalit' means 'suppressed and exploited people'. The concept
seems to have emerged from the people's usage in Maharashtra.
The term 'Dalit' became really popular only after the emergence of
the 'Dalit Panthers' movement in Maharashtra in the 1970s. 'Dalit'
as it is usually understood encompasses only the so-called
untouchable castes. Though recently some organizations like the
Dalit Maha Sabha of Andhra Pradesh did attempt to use the word
'Dalit' to denote SCs, STs (Scheduled Tribes) and OBCs, the popular
press and the masses themselves never took up the usage.

Meanwhile from 1984 onwards the concept of 'Bahujan' began to
become popular with the emergence of the Bahujan Samaj party
(BSP). Kanshi Ram, the national president of the BSP, began to use

the term 'Bahujans', to refer to SCs, STs and OBCs. He also expressed the view that one should not use the term 'Dalit' as it separates SCs from STs and OBCs. The concept 'Bahujan' simply means 'majority'. It is in this sense that the term was first used by Buddha and then by Phule. The problem is that it does not point to what the nature of that majority population is. To resolve the problem, I have decided to use the term 'Dalitbahujans' to refer to SCs and OBCs. One may also, as Kanshi Ram does, include the STs in it. But I have not discussed STs in this book as strictly speaking they do not figure in the caste system.

The concept 'Dalitbahujan' as I have used it in this book means 'people and castes who form the exploited and suppressed majority'. I am aware that there are contradictions among the many castes that are referred to by this term. At the same time, I am also aware that there are cultural and economic commonalities as well as commonalities of productive knowledge which mesh them together like threads in a cloth.

I hope, therefore, that in a struggle to liberate themselves from caste and class exploitation and oppression, the Dalitbahujans turn to the base of the material culture to emerge as a united force. Over a period of time the brahminical castes will become casteless and classless and then we will establish an egalitarian India. In the subtitle of the book, however, I have retained the word 'Sudra' so that the readers can easily understand where the critique has come from.

Hyderabad, 5 February 1995

Introduction

I was born in a small South Indian Telangana village in the early 1950s and grew up in the 1960s. Our villages had undergone all the turbulence of the freedom movement as they were part of a historical struggle known as the Telangana Armed Struggle. Perhaps as part of the first generation that was born and brought up in post-colonial India, an account of my childhood experiences would also be a narrative of the cultural contradictions that we are undergoing. Village India has not changed radically from my childhood days to the present. If there are any changes, the changes are marginal. Urban India is only an extension of village India. There is a cultural continuum between village India and urban India.

Suddenly, since about 1990 the word 'Hindutva' has begun to echo in our ears, day in and day out, as if everyone in India who is not a Muslim, a Christian or a Sikh is a Hindu. Suddenly I am being told that I am a Hindu. I am also told that my parents, relatives and the caste in which we were born and brought up are Hindu. This totally baffles me. In fact, the whole cultural milieu of the urban middle class—the newspapers that I read, the T.V. that I see—keeps assaulting me, morning and evening, forcing me to declare that I am a Hindu. Otherwise I am socially castigated and my environment is vitiated. Having been born in a Kurumaa (shepherd caste) family, I do not know how I can relate to the Hindu culture that is being projected through all kinds of advertising agencies. The government and the state themselves have become big advertising agencies. Moreover the Sangh Parivar harasses us every day by calling us Hindus. In fact, the very sight of its saffron-tilak culture is a harassment to us.

The question before me now is not whether I must treat Muslims or Christians or Sikhs as enemies, as the Hindutva school wants me to do. The question is What do we, the lower Sudras and Ati-Sudras (whom I also call Dalitbahujans), have to do with Hinduism or with Hindutva itself? I, indeed not only I, but all of us, the Dalitsbahujans of India, have never heard the word 'Hindu'—not as a word, nor as the name of a culture, nor as the name of a religion in our early childhood days. We heard about *Turukoollu* (Muslims), we heard about *Kirastaanapoollu* (Christians), we heard about *Baapanocllu* (Brahmins) and *Koomatoollu* (Baniyas) spoken of as people who were different from us. Among these four categories, the most different were the Baapanoollu and the Koomatoollu. There are at least some aspects of life common to us and the Turukoollu and Kirastaanapoollu. We all eat meat, we all touch each other. With the Turukoollu, we shared several other cultural relations. We both celebrated the *Peerila* festival. Many Turukoollu came with us to the fields. The only people with whom we had no relations, whatsoever, were the Baapanoollu and the Koomatoollu. But today we are suddenly being told that we have a common religious and cultural relationship with the Baapanoollu and the Koomatoollu. This is not merely surprising; it is shocking.

EXPERIENCE AS FRAMEWORK

It is for this reason that I thought I should examine the socio-economic and cultural differences between us and the Brahmins, the Kshatriyas and the Baniyas. The socio-cultural differences would be better understood if we set them in the context of the different stages of our lives—childhood, family life, market relations, power relations, the Gods and Goddesses that we respect, death, and so on. Narratives of personal experiences are the best contexts in which to compare and contrast these social forms. Personal experience brings out reality in a striking way. This method of examining socio-cultural and economic history is central to the social sciences; significantly, the method of narrating and deconstructing experiences has been used by feminists. Further, Indian Dalitbahujan thinkers like Mahatma Phule, Ambedkar and Periyar E. V. Ramasamy have also used this method. Instead of depending on Western methods, Phule, Ambedkar and Periyar spoke and wrote on the day-to-day experiences of the Dalitbahujan castes. I would argue that this is the only possible and indeed the most authentic way in which the deconstruction and reconstruction of history can take place.

Certainly there are problems in contrasting our own experiences, with the experiences of the 'others'—the Brahmins and the Baniyas. This becomes more problematic in a society like ours in which the Dalitbahujan castes and the Hindu castes (Brahmins, Baniyas, Kshatriyas and neo-Kshatriyas) may live in one village, but the Hindu 'upper' caste culture is completely closed to the Dalitbahujan castes. In this respect I am exceptionally fortunate because after I joined Osmania University I made many friends—particularly feminists— who came from Brahmin families. I had long discussions with many of them. My association with the Dalit and civil rights movements helped me understand both the cultures in some depth. I have, therefore, tried to analyse, critique and problematize many popular notions in this small book. Let me make it clear, however, that I am not writing this book to convince suspicious brahminical minds; I am writing this book for all those who have open minds. My request to Brahmin, Baniya and Neo-Kshatriya intellectuals is this: For about three thousand years you people learnt only how to teach and what to teach others—the Dalitbahujans. Now in your own interest and in the interest of this great country you must learn to listen and to read what we have to say. A people who refuse to listen to new questions and learn new answers will perish and not prosper.

CHAPTER 1

Childhood Formations

WHY I AM NOT A HINDU

I was not born a Hindu for the simple reason that my parents did not know that they were Hindus. This does not mean that I was born as a Muslim, a Christian, a Buddhist, a Sikh or a Parsee. My illiterate parents, who lived in a remote South Indian village, did not know that they belonged to any religion at all. People belong to a religion only when they know that they are part of the people who worship that God, when they go to those temples and take part in the rituals and festivals of that religion. My parents had only one identity and that was their caste: they were Kurumaas. Their festivals were local, their Gods and Goddesses were local, and sometimes these were even specific to one village. No centralized religious symbols existed for them. This does not mean they were tribals. My ancestors took to life on the plains about 500 years ago. They were integrated into the village economy, paid taxes to the village panchayat or to the state administration in whichever form the administration required. As long as they were shepherds, they paid the tax in the form of *pullara* (levy for sheep-breeding). In the years before I was born, they shifted the occupation from sheep-breeding to agriculture and paid land rent to the local landlord and to the tehesil office. Even in my childhood I remember my parents paying taxes both for sheep-breeding and for cultivating the land. But they never paid a religion tax, something which all feudal religions normally demand. Not only that, they never went to a temple in which they could meet villagers belonging to all castes. In fact, there was no temple where all the village people could meet on a regular basis.

This does not mean that my family alone was excluded from the religious process because it was a family that could be ignored or neglected. Not so. For two generations my ancestors had been the caste heads. My mother and her mother-in-law (that is, my grandmother) were members of a leading family of the Kurumaa caste. In the village economy, Kurumaas, Gollaas, Goudaas, Kapuus, Shalaas, Chakaalies, Mangalies and Maadigaas, formed the majority in terms of numbers. The entire village economy was governed by the daily operations of these castes.

CULTURAL DIFFERENCES BETWEEN
THE HINDUS AND US

Let me now narrate how my childhood experiences were shaped. The social structure in which I first became conscious of the world around me was a Kurumaa social structure. My playmates, friends, and of course relatives, all belonged to the Kurumaa caste. Occasionally the friendship circle extended to Goudaa boys and Kaapu boys. We were friends because we were all part of the cattle-breeding youth. We took the cattle to the field and then began playing *chirra gone* (our cricket), *gooleelu* (a game with marbles), *dongaata* (a hide-and-seek game), and so on. Surprisingly, whenever a Goudaa friend came to my house he would eat with us, but sit slightly apart; when we went to Kaapu homes their parents would give us food but make us sit a little distance away. While eating we were not supposed to touch each other. But later we could play together and drink together from the rivers and streams. If we had carried our mid-day food to the cattle field, we sometimes attempted to touch each other's food, but suddenly the rules that our parents had fixed would make their appearance: we would speak insultingly of each others' castes and revert to eating separately. Within moments, however, we were together again.

Agriculture being a collective activity of the village, the cows, bulls and buffaloes were commonly owned as property of many castes. This was perhaps a meeting ground for the village economy. Thus when we went along with cattle, social life on the cattle ground became an inter-caste affair. But as we grew up, this life we had in common and the shared consciousness began splitting even in terms of production relations. I and my Kurumaa friends withdrew from common cattle-tending activities and were trained in sheep-breeding, which is a specific occupation of Kurumaas and Gollaas alone. At the same time, my Goudaa friends were drawn into their toddy-tapping and Kaapu friends into plough-driving.

THE CASTE TRAINING OF BOYS

Each one of us was supposed to pick up the language of our particular caste. I was introduced to the specific language of sheep and sheep-rearing tasks. I was taught the different names of the sheep—*bolli gorre, pulla gorre, nalla gorre,* and so on. I learnt about the diseases that the sheep were afflicted with, how a delivery should be 'midwifed', how young ones should be handled, which was the best green grass for rearing the sheep. Goats required special treatment as they were to be fed with tree leaves (goats do not eat grass). We learnt what herbal medicines should be applied when sheep and goats are attacked by diseases. If the diseases were nerve-based ones, we learnt how to touch the sheep with a hot iron rod at the relevant place. One of the most difficult and expert tasks was shearing the wool from the sheep's body. The scissors had to be handled with such care that they cut close but did not cut the skin of the sheep. All this was part of the expertise of a sheep-rearer, and we were carefully educated in all these tasks.

THE CASTE TRAINING OF GIRLS

How were the girls being educated or brought up? Whether they were my sisters or others, the pattern of training was the same. The elder girls were taught, even as they turned three, how to handle a younger brother or sister. Holding a three-month-old baby requires skill and care, more so when the arms are those of a three-year-old girl. This was the most important help that the mother needed when she left home for sheep-related activities or agrarian work, early in the morning. Mothers would also teach them how to powder chillies, husk the paddy, sweep the home, and clean the eating bowls.

Besides this, a Kurumaa woman teaches her daughter how to separate the wool from the thorns that stick to it and to prepare it for thread-making (*taadu wadakadam*). All these tasks are extremely skilled. By the age of twelve or thirteen (by the time she has reached puberty) a Kurumaa girl is supposed to know the basics of cooking. She begins with lighting the hearth and learning to handle it. A Kurumaa hearth consists of three stones with an extension on one side. On this extension stands a pot, known as a *vothu,* on which water is kept boiling. It requires a special skill not to upset or crack the vothu while cooking on the main hearth. Kurumaa girls also learn how to manage the *kuraadu* which is an important part of Kurumaa cooking (as it is of all other Dalitbahujan castes). A Kurumaa kuraadu consists of *ganji* (starch), drained from cooked rice and then left to ferment slightly until it gives out a mild sour smell. While cooking rice or *jawar,* the kuraadu is invariably used as the liquid *(yesaru).* Kuraadu is considered good for health, in addition, it drives away evil spirits from the food. Every girl is initiated into these skills at an early age. First of all, handling pots that are vulnerable to breaking requires care and cultivated skill. The only activity that was not taught to our girls which an urban girl might have to learn today was washing clothes. This is because washing was the washerman/woman's task. A girl born in a Chakaali (washerman) family learns all these activities in addition to learning how to wash various kinds of clothes.

The girls of these families are also taught, at an young age, how to seed the furrow by carefully dropping seed after seed. They are taught how to weed and even out extra growth in the crop; they learn how to plant with bent backs, moving backwards in the muddy land. Quite a lot of explanation by the adults go into the teaching of these activities to the young ones. Invariably there are experts in each activity who acquire a name for themselves. Young people are proud to emulate such experts.

SEXUAL MORES

Sexual behaviour and mores are also taught as part of family and peer group life. A girl listens to older women talking to each other in groups about 'disciplined' women and 'indisciplined' women; their sexual life-styles, their relations with husbands and others. A father does not hesitate to talk in front of his children about his approach to life or his relations with other women. More important than the father's is the mother's approach towards the children. A Dalitbahujan mother trains her children as a hen trains the chickens. She takes the children along with her to the fields, and sets them very small tasks in the field. While walking to the fields she often shares her problems with the children, particularly with the girls. It is not unconventional for her to talk to them about every aspect of her life.

If any Dalitbahujan woman has a relationship with a man who is not her husband, the relationship does not remain a secret. The entire *waada* discusses it. Even the children of that family come to know about it. Particularly when the father and mother quarrel, every aspect of life becomes public. No quarrel hides inside the house. For the children the house is a place of pleasure and of pain but it is all in the open. Male children learn about women and about sex in the company of their friends, in the cattle-rearing grounds or sheep-feeding fields. All kind of sexual trials take place in the fields. The 'bad' and 'good' of life are learnt at quite an early stage. Each one of these practices are discussed in terms of its morality and immorality. But this morality and immorality is not based on a divine order or divine edict. It is discussed in terms of the harmony of the families.

CASE LANGUAGE

Caste language is structured by its own grammar. It is a flexible and alert grammar, designed for production-based communication. Though it has developed without the help of writing, it is no less so-phisticated than 'standard' brahminical Telugu. Children's experience of language begins with fixing the names of things—birds, animals, trees, insects, everything that is around them. Every tree, every in-sect, every living and non-living being bears a name. Many of these things do not have words for them in 'standard' brahminical language. Brahminical language does not understand our ways of making-up new names. These names are not taught through the written word but are orally repeated in communication that is use-based.

Each caste is rooted in its productive process and its language is structured around that production. The Kurumaas have their own language as do the Lambadaas, the Erukalaas or the Koyaas. The Kurumaas not only know about the sheep, goats, trees, plants, and so on, they know the names of every instrument used in wool-making and blanket-weaving. A Goudaa knows the names of a whole range of instruments, skills and activities that are required for toddy-tapping. The specialization that one acquires in communicating these caste occupational tasks is as much or more sophisticated than that possessed by a Brahmin who utters the several names of his Gods while reciting a mantra. What is ironical is that the recitation of several names of one God or many Gods is construed as wisdom, whereas knowing the language of production and the names of productive tools is not recognized as knowledge. The Brahmins have defined knowledge in their own image. But the fact still remains that each caste has built a treasure house of its own knowledge and its own vocabulary. Each caste has built its own special consciousness. As individuals we acquire a consciousness of ourselves, our environment, our production and procreation. This consciousness has nothing to do with organized religion. Further, language here is a social instrument of communication and of the expression of that particular consciousness.

OUR GODS AND CONSCIOUSNESS

What further separated a Hindu from us was the nature of the consciousness of the other world, the divine and the spiritual. For children from our castes, *Jeja* (the concept of God) is introduced in the form of the moon. As children grow up, they also get acquainted with Pochamma, Polimeramma, Kattamaisamma, Kaatamaraju, Potaraju and other deities. Among Dalitbahujans, there is no concept of a temple in a definite place or form. Goddesses and Gods live in all forms and in all shapes and in different places. Every Dalitbahujan child learns at an early age about these Goddesses and Gods. The children are part of the caste congregations that take place during festivals such as Bonaalu, Chinna Panduga, Pedda Panduga, and so on. Every Dalitbahujan child learns at an early age that smallpox comes because Pochamma is angry. The rains are late because Polimeramma is angry. The village tank gets filled or does not get filled depending on the sympathies of Kattamaisamma. Crops are stolen by thieves because Potaraju is angry. For Kurumaas whether sheep and goats will prosper depends on the attitude of Beerappa, a caste-specific God. Thus there are common village Dalitbahujan Gods and Goddesses and caste-specific Gods and Goddesses. Of course, for us the spirit exists, the *atma* (soul) exists, dead people come back to re-live in our own surroundings in the form of ghosts if they have not been fed well while they were alive. But there is no *swarga* (heaven) and there is no *naraka* (hell). All the dead live together somewhere in the skies. This consciousness has not yet taken the shape of an organized religion. The Dalitbahujan spirit in its essence is a non-Hindu spirit because the Hindu patriarchal Gods do not exist among us at all.

We knew nothing of Brahma, Vishnu or Eswara until we entered school. When we first heard about these figures they were as strange to us as Allah or Jehova or Jesus were. Even the name of Buddha, about whom we later learnt of as a mobilizer of Dalitbahujans against brahminical ritualism, was not known to us.

The language that a Brahmin, Baniya or Kshatriya child learns to speak, all the social relationships that these children were supposed to be picking up as part of Hindu culture, were also alien to us. I have later learnt and observed that a Brahmin child is not taught to go to the field, or to look after the cattle or crops, but is supposed to go to school at an early age. Many of my Brahmin friends have told me that a traditional Brahmin father never touches his children. Child-rearing is essentially a wife's burden. Washing a child is seen as unclean activity and hence it is left to the woman. While the mother looks after the child, does the so-called upper caste father help in the kitchen? No. The kitchen too is a dirty place which he should not enter. Thus the brahminical notion of purity and pollution operates even at home. In contrast to our skill-based vocabulary they learn words like Veda, *Ramayana, Mahabharatha,* Purana, and so on. At an early age they hear names like Brahma, Vishnu, Rama, Krishna, Lakshmi, Saraswathi, Sita and Savithri. Their children are told the stories of these Gods' heroism (mostly killing) and the Goddesses' femininity. Vishnu, for example, is shown to be reclining on a serpent, with Lakshmi at his feet, pressing them.

Even a Brahmin family might talk about Pochamma, Maisamma or Ellamma, but not with the same respect as they would about Brahma, Vishnu, Maheswara. For them Pochamma and Maisamma are 'Sudra' Goddesses and supposed to be powerful but in bad, negative ways. A Pochamma according to them does not demand the respect that Lakshmi or Saraswathi do, because Lakshmi and Saraswathi are supposed to be ideal wives of ideal husbands, whereas no one knows who Pochamma's husband is, any more than they can name Maisamma's husband. This is the reason why even if a Brahmin invokes the name of Pochamma when there is smallpox in his house, it is only in a derogatory way. No Brahmin or Baniya child bears the name of Pochamma, Maisamma or Ellamma. Whereas in our families Pochamma, Maisamma and Ellamma are revered names and we name our children after these Goddesses. In Dalitbahujan families Pochamma and Maisamma are Goddesses revered in their own capacity. It does not strike an average Dalitbahujan consciousness that these Goddesses do not have husbands and hence need to be spoken of derogatorily. This is because there are many widows in our villages who are highly respected, whose stature is based on their skills at work and their approach towards fellow human beings. I remember many young widows in my village who were the team leaders of agrarian operations as they were the most respected persons.

Between the people and Pochamma there is no priest. In fact there is no need of a priest at all in the worship of our Gods and Goddesses. Even as children we used to appeal to her to be kind to us so that we would not fall prey to smallpox or fever. As children we never thought that these Gods and Goddesses did not understand our language or that we needed a priest to talk to God in Sanskrit. Like our parents, who appealed to these Gods and Goddesses in our own language, we too appealed to them in our native tongues. We related ourselves to these Goddesses in a variety of ways.

A Hindu family is hierarchical. Girls must obey boys, children must obey elders. Sex and age are two determining and measuring rods of the status within the family. Children are trained not to get involved in production-related tasks, which Brahmins condemn as 'Sudra' tasks. Similarly their friendship with Dalitbahujan children is censured. 'Upper' castes speak of Dalitbahujans as 'ugly'. 'Sudra' is an abusive word; 'Chandala' is a much more abusive word. 'Upper' caste children are taught to live differently from Dalitbahujan children, just as they are taught to despise and dismiss them. Hindu inhumanism becomes part of their early formation; hating others—the Dalitbahujans—is a part of their consciousness.

Discussion of sexual behaviour is a taboo in Hindu families. Mothers are not supposed to talk to daughters about their sexual experiences. The father's atrocities against the mother cannot be discussed in Brahmin or Baniya families. But this is not so in our families. The father abuses the mother right in front of the children and the mother will pay back in the same coin then and there. The children are a witness to all that. In Hindu families the father can abuse the mother, but the mother is not supposed to retort. A wife is supposed to put up with all the atrocities that a husband commits against her; the more a wife puts up with the husband's atrocities the more she is appreciated. In addition, brahminical 'upper' castes teach their children about the need for *madi* (wearing a wet cloth on one's body to remain 'pure' while cooking). The cooking of food must take place according to ritual modes. Each girl is taught to cook according to the tastes of the male members. A dozen curries must be cooked as part of the Brahmin *bhojanam*. Every girl is supposed to know that every Brahmin male's good eating is equivalent to God's good eating. If there are poor Brahmins and even if they can only afford a few items, those items must be prepared in terms of their relation to God. In these families God and men are equated in many respects. But in our families the situation is very different.

MAADIGAAS AND HINDUS

Let us turn to the Maadigaas, whom the Hindutva school claims as part of their religion. My village used to have about 40 Maadigaa families who lived adjacent to the locality of the Goudaas. These two castes had no relations of touching with each other. In my village, I do not recall ever having had a childhood Maadigaa friend. The Maadigaa boys who were younger than me were *jeetaas* (farm servants). Their family and cultural relations were very similar to ours. But what was different was that from childhood they were taught to be always fearfully obedient, addressing the young and the old of the so-called upper castes as *ayya baanchan*. While they were jeetas, at the age of five, they were supposed to look after the cattle and the buffaloes and watch the crops. Their childhood was much tougher than ours. But in certain areas they were far more skilled and intelligent. They knew how to skin dead cattle, convert the skin into soft and smooth leather and transform the leather into farm instruments and shoes. Their skill in playing the *dappu* (a special percussion instrument) was far beyond that of any one of us. Maadigaa boys and girls were taught, right from childhood, and as a matter of their daily survival, to be humble before the landlord, Brahmin and Koomati.

The same is true of the Chakaali and Mangali children. At home they live as equals, eating, drinking and smoking together. They are equals from childhood onwards. The father and the mother teach children these things as part of their education. Equality and morality are not two different entities for parents and children. They teach the children that 'they must shiver and shake before the "upper" caste master'. This is not because the Maadigaa, Chakaali and Mangali parents have great respect or real love for the 'upper' caste landlord, the Brahmin or the Baniya, but because there is always the fear of losing their jobs. They will say, 'My son, be careful with that bastard, pretend to be very obedient, otherwise that rascal will hit us in our stomachs.' The child pretends to be obedient as Gandhi pretended to be poor. But a pretence that starts at an early age becomes part of a person's behaviour during a lifetime. Fear of the 'upper' caste *dora* is gradually internalized. Every Dalitbahujan family that teaches children about equality at home also teaches them about hierarchical life in society for the simple reason that otherwise terrible atrocities may follow. Except for the fact that they are made untouchables, except for their appalling economic conditions, the Maadigaas are absolutely like the

Kurumaas, the Goudaas and others. There is less religiosity among them than in any other castes. If the Kurumaas, Goudaas, Kapuus and Shalaas have seven or eight Goddesses and Gods, the Maadigaas have one or two. They play the dappu for every occasion, but in a total participatory way they celebrate only the festival of Ellamma who is their *kuladevi* (caste Goddess). For them even hell and heaven do not exist. Each day, earning the food for that day is at the heart of their life struggle. A day without food is hell and a day with food, heaven.

Among all these castes what was unknown was reading the book, going to the temple, chanting prayers or doing the *sandhyaavandanam* (evening worship). The Bhagavad Gita is said to be a Hindu religious text. But that book was not supposed to enter our homes. Not only that, the Hindu religion and its Brahmin wisdom prohibited literacy to all of us. Till modern education and Ambedkar's theory of reservation created a small educated section among these castes, letter-learning was literally prohibited. This was a sure way of not letting the religious text enter our lives. In addition even the idol or *murthy-based*, priest or pujari-centred temple was prohibited to the young, the adult and the old from the Dalitbahujan castes. Today, though some 'lower' castes are allowed into temples they can never relate to that God or Goddess.

SCHOOL EDUCATION

As the first generation in Dalitbahujan history to see a slate and a pencil, we jumped straight out of the jungle into school. Even there, what was there in common between the Hindus and us? The Brahmin-Baniya children are the privileged. They are better dressed and better fed. Though they are born in the same village, the children enter the school with different cultures. Our eating habits are not the same. For all Dalitbahujans good food means meat and fish. We enjoy it, we relish it. For Brahmin-Baniya boys and girls even a discussion about meat and fish makes them feel like vomiting. For Maadigaas and Muslims beef is an item to be relished; though for us it was prohibited, we never hated it as the Brahmin-Baniyas did. These differences are not the differences of individual tastes, they are differences created as part of our upbringing.

Our school teacher's attitude to each one of us depended on his own caste background. If he was a Brahmin he hated us and told us to our faces that it was because of the evil time—because of *kaliyuga*, that he was being forced to teach 'Sudras' like us. In his view we were good for nothing. That 'wise' teacher used to think of us as coming from *suudari* families (families of field hands). Working in the field in his view was dirty and unaesthetic. According to him only mad people would work in dirty, muddy fields. Today we realize it was good that we were muddy. We realize that mud is the birthplace of food and of the working people's ideas.

But who, according to the teachers, were the great ones? The children who came from Brahmin, Baniya and of course the 'upper' caste landlord families. These were the 'great' ones. Because they did not do dirty farm work, their faces were cleanly washed, their clothes were cleaner, their hair carefully oiled and combed. They came to school wearing chappals, whereas those who feed cattle and those who make chappals from the skin of the cattle do not have chappals to wear. These were the reasons why we were ignorant, ugly and unclean. It is not merely the teacher, even 'upper' caste school children think about Dalitbahujan children that way.

As we were growing up, stepping into higher classes, the textbooks taught us stories which we had never heard in our families. The stories of Rama and Krishna, poems from the Puranas, the names of two epics called *Ramayana* and *Mahabharatha* occurred repeatedly. Right from early school up to college, our Telugu textbooks were packed with these Hindu stories. For Brahmin-Baniya students these were their childhood stories, very familiar not only in the story form but in the form of the Gods that they worshipped. Whenever they went to temples with their parents they saw the images of these *devataas*. The boys bore the names of these Gods; the girls the names of the Goddesses. I distinctly remember how alien all these names appeared to me. Many of the names were not known in my village. The name of Kalidasa was as alien to us as the name of Shakespeare. The only difference was that one appeared in Telugu textbooks while the other appeared in English textbooks. Perhaps for the Brahmin-Baniya students the situation was different. The language of textbooks was not the one that our communities spoke. Even the basic words were different. Textbook Telugu was Brahmin Telugu, whereas we were used to a production-based communicative Telugu. In a word, our alienation from the Telugu textbook was more or less the same as it was from the English textbook in terms of language and content. It is not merely a difference of dialect; there is difference in the very language itself.

To date I have not come across a Telugu textbook which is written in this production-based, communicative language. I have not come across a lesson on Pochamma, Potaraju, Kattamaisamma, Kaatamaraju or Beerappa. This is not because these Gods and Goddesses do not have narratives associated with them. Without such narratives they would never have survived for thousands of years among the people. If we listen to Dalitbahujan story-tellers telling these stories, they keep us spellbound. The simple reason is that no writer—and the majority of writers happen to be Brahmins—thought that these stories could be written down so that they could go into school and college textbooks. In their view the very names of our Goddesses and Gods are not worth mentioning.

No mainstream Telugu poet ever thought that going down to the people's culture means talking about these Goddesses and Gods too. No poet thought that what people talk about, discuss and communicate with each other every day makes poetry. Even poets and writers who were born in these Hindu families and later turned Communist, atheist or rationalist, they too never picked up the contents of our daily lives as their subjects. Ironically even the names of those revolutionary leaders sounded alien to us. For them, Yellaiah, Pullaiah, Buchaiah, Buchamma, Lachamma were names of the Other. And the Other need never become the subject of their writings or the centre of their narratives.

The purohits praised the Puranas and the Communist and rationalist writers wrote critiques of these Puranas. But nobody thought that we too have a soul and that that soul needs to be talked about. Nobody thought that there are Pochamma, Maisamma and Potaraju who need to be talked about too. Even the Communists and rationalists spoke and wrote in the language of the purohit himself.

Their culture was basically Sanskritized; we were not part of that culture. For good or ill, no one talked about us. They never realized that our language is also a language, that it is understood by one and all in our communities; not to forget the fact that these communities are not small in number; they are made up of lakhs and crores whereas the Hindu 'upper' castes are few in number. If our parents had been conscious about the conspiracy of this silent violence, they would have simply inhaled all the Hindus as *nasham* (like they usually inhale tobacco powder). What was arrested and what was stifled was that consciousness. The consciousness of 'us' and of 'our' culture was never allowed to exercise our minds.

Childhood formations are important for a person—female or male—to become a full human being. But our childhoods were mutilated by constant abuse and by silence, and by a stunning silence at that. There was the conspiracy to suppress the formation of our consciousness. For hundreds of generations the violent stoppage of the entry of the written word into our homes and our lives nipped our consciousness in the very bud. Even after schools were opened to us because of independence or *swaraj,* a word which even today I fail to understand, the school teacher was against us, the textbook language was against us. Our homes have one culture and the schools have another culture. If our culture was Dalitbahujan, the culture of the school was Hindu. The gap between the two was enormous. There was no way in which one resembled the other. In fact these two cultures were poles apart.

What difference did it make to us whether we had an English textbook that talked about Milton's *Paradise Lost* or *Paradise Regained,* or Shakespeare's *Othello* or *Macbeth* or Wordsworth's poetry about nature in England, or a Telugu textbook which talked about Kalidasa's *Meghasandesham*, Bommera Potanna's *Bhagavatam*, or Nannaya and Tikkana's *Mahabharatham* except the fact that one textbook is written with twenty-six letters and the other in fifty-six letters? We do not share the contents of either; we do not find our lives reflected in their narratives. We cannot locate our family settings in them. In none of these books do we find words that are familiar to us. Without the help of a dictionary neither makes any sense to us. How does it make any difference to us whether it is Greek and Latin that are written in Roman letters or Sanskrit that is written in Telugu?

Right from school 'their' male children talked about 'their' initiation into the Hindu religion through the *upanayana*. From the day after the upanayana a white thread hangs around their bodies, and from then on they are known as twice-born, thus more pure and superior, whereas we always remain once-born. When we first heard about the upanayana, we too desired to wear such a thread. It is a different thing that many of us would have later thrown that thread into muddy waters as Basava did at the early age of twelve. But the fact is that at the age of seven or eight, if there had been an occasion when we became the focal point of the house and a priest came to initiate us into religion, we would have gained confidence. Not only that, when we learnt that in the Brahmin, Baniya and other 'upper' caste families, initiation into writing takes place at the age of four and that it is also a festive occasion, how much we resented it!

In the olden days, after such initiation, the so-called upper castes used to send their sons to *gurukulas* (brahminical schools). Now they send them to English-medium convent schools; the very schools that were hated by the same Hindus during the freedom struggle. Even in the 1990s Hindutva ideologues condemn such schools as 'anti-Hindutva' schools—of course, only to send their children into the same schools promptly after the upanayana. The Hindus condemn English, yet they send their children to English-medium schools. We have not yet acquired the consciousness to condemn the complete domination of Telugu-medium schools by the Hindu scriptures. Having had no alternative we send our children to schools that teach only the Puranas, or the epics in every textbook. This is a paradox, and we live with many such paradoxes.

When we were told that Hindu girls and boys were married even when they were children, we thought of these practices as familiar since child marriage was also part of our lives. But when we read in the textbooks that the girls whose husbands died must remain widows and have their heads shaved; that they were to be clad only in white, we found it strange. In our families, girls whose in-laws did not look after them well, got divorced very easily and within days second husbands were found for them. While marriages take place at home and are celebrated with one type of meal and drink, divorces also take place with food and drink. Seeking divorce from an irresponsible husband is as much a sanctioned social act as performing marriages. In my childhood, when I read about Savithri struggling against the death of her husband, because otherwise she would become a widow, I was very happy that our women do not have to struggle like her.

Similarly, when we read that Hindu women ought to die along with their dead husbands I was extremely happy that our women do not have to die like that. I was so glad that we do not belong to such a religion because if suddenly my father were to die my mother would not have to die also. If she so desired she could get me a stepfather. What about history textbooks and Telugu textbooks that told us story after story about women who committed *sati* but there was not a single lesson about our women who still lived after their husbands' deaths, who worked, brought up their children and got them married? There was not a single lesson about women who found it difficult to get a divorce and had to struggle hard to make that divorce actually take place. There was not a single lesson which talked about the parents who had to struggle hard to get their daughter married three times or four times because husband after husband turned out to be a bad person. Not a single textbook gave us moral lessons that there were brave parents who never wanted to let down their daughters. The textbook morality was different from our living morality.

In all these stories and lessons we read about ideal men and women and of cultures that were very different from ours. In the Hindu texts, a knowledgeable man was one who knows the Vedas, a courageous person was one who kills enemies—even if the enemies are friends and relatives. In the *Ramayana* and the *Mahabharatha*, knowledge and courage were defined in these terms. But in our real life a knowledgeable person is one who has knowledge of social functions—one who knows about sheep-breeding, agriculture, rope making; one who can diagnose the nature of the diseases of animals and human beings. A courageous person is one who can fight tigers, lions, snakes, wild bulls; who can travel deep into forests, swim the rivers and find the missing goats and sheep.

HINDU IDEALS AND OUR IDEALS

In Brahmin *waadas* and families, narratives about heroes and heroines do not exist within a human context. This is because Brahmin life is alienated from the kind of socioeconomic environment in which a real hero or a heroine can be constructed. Their social settings are the reading of *slokaas* or mantras with proficiency. The greatest achievement is learning the whole of the *Ramayana* or the *Mahabharatha* or the Bhagvad Gita by heart. Womanhood is discussed in terms of devotion to the husband and cooking with purity and pollution in mind. In fact brahminical culture eulogizes negative heroes and negative heroines. For example, Krishna who encourages one to kill one's own relatives is a hero. Arjuna who killed his relatives is a hero. In these narratives acquiring private property (the whole of the *Mahabharatha* is constructed around land becoming the private property of minorities, who are not involved in production) is idealized.

In 'Sudra' waadas it is just the opposite. There are a number of real-life situations from which ideal heroes and heroines emerge. Their daily working interaction with nature provides the scope for their formation. One who kills relatives, for whatever reason, and one who commits crimes, for whatever reason, becomes a crook. One who encourages killing is not a God but a devil worth condemning. A Pochamma did not become our heroine because she killed somebody, a Kattamaisamma did not become our heroine because she killed somebody; a Beerappa did not become our hero because he killed somebody. They became our heroines and heroes because they saved us from diseases, or from hunger, and so on. Hindu morality is just the opposite of our living morality. Take another example. An ideal woman in a Hindu text is one who does not eat and drink in the presence of older women and men of all ages. A woman is not supposed to smoke and drink even if the man is a chain-smoker and the worst drunkard. But in our homes no one talks badly about a woman who smokes or has a drink. All our women drink toddy or liquor along with our men. Our women smoke *chuttaas* (cigars made with leaves and tobacco) at home and in the fields. They try to be at least notionally equal to men in all respects.

Those who say that all of us are Hindus must tell us which morality is Hindu morality? Which values do they want to uphold as right values? The 'upper' caste Hindu unequal and inhuman cultural values or our cultural values? What is the ideal of society today? What shall we teach the children of today? Shall we teach them what has been taught by the Hindus or what the Dalitbahujan masses of this country want to learn? Who makes an ideal teacher? Who becomes a good hero? One who produces varieties of crops, one who faces lions and tigers or one who kills the relatives and friends, simply because what 'upper' castes think is *dharma* and others think is *adharma?* Where do we begin and where do we end? We must begin by creating our history and we must end by changing this very social fabric.

The Brahmin-Baniyas think that their non-productive ritualistic life is great and the Dalitbahujan non-ritualistic working life is mean. This philosophical make-up moulds the child population of these two communities differently. The Brahmin-Baniya 'upper' caste children think that they are the greater race, and that they are better bred. All this was proclaimed so consistently that it went into our psyches as if it might be true. Thus Brahminism consolidated its own socio-cultural position in society. Since our parents have been denied education, which alone could have enabled them to assess their own position realistically, whatever social status the Brahmin, parading as an *ayyagaaru,* assigned to our parents, they passed on to us. Right from childhood, in spite of the fact that we had such great skills, we remained diffident. Once Brahminism had unnerved human beings who were so much mightier and powerful, the diffidence was passed on from generation to generation. The whole lot of us—the whole Dalitbahujan population—were made to see things upside down.

Brahmin-Baniya temples were not only far from us, but the Gods sitting and sleeping in those temples were basically set against us. There were Brahmin-Baniya houses within our villages, but the very same houses built up a culture inimical to ours. The Brahmin-Baniyas walked over the corpses of our culture. They were the gluttons while our parents were the poor starving people—producing everything for the Other's comfort. Their children were the most unskilled gluttons, whereas our children were the contributors to the national economy itself. Their notion of life was unworthy of life itself, but they repeatedly told our parents that we were the most useless people. Having gone through all these stages of life, having acquired the education that enabled us to see a wider world, when we reflect upon our childhood and its processes it is nothing but anger and anguish which keep burning in our hearts.

CHAPTER 2

Marriage, Market and Social Relations

MARRIAGE

Marriage is as important in our families as it is in Hindu families. But in form and content it is different from that of Brahmin-Baniya marriages. For us, marriage is a human and a worldly affair that performs the human functions of production and procreation. This is clear from a proverb that our people use very frequently: *janta leenidee panta pandadi* ('without the couple, how can there be a crop?'). For Hindus, marriage is a sacred ritual divorced from all kinds of productive activity even notionally. Even in procreation the main intention is to produce a son who can pave the father's way to heaven. Holding the *talagooru* (a water pot carried in front of a dead body) and performing the *shraaddha* (the last rites) are not simply rituals done at the instance of the priest who visits the household only on such occasions as marriage and death, they are part of the very making of a brahminical Hindu self. The situation is not the same in Dalitbahujan families.

In Kurumaa families, marriage is contracted with the involvement of the whole caste. Neither *kanya shulkam* (bride price) nor *varakatnam* (groom price) play an important role. Of course, child marriage has, over a period of time, become part of the marriage system. But the story of Beerappa indicates that love marriage was the caste norm of the Kurumaas. It was to preserve that norm of love marriage that he fought battles with his maternal uncle.

However these caste societies have also degenerated and love marriage has gone out of existence even among them. Love marriage no longer exists as an accepted form. The common practice has degenerated to the level of child marriage. But a careful observation of instruments that each caste uses on the occasion of marriage indicates that production is the focal point. In the marriage *laggarn* (main part of the marriage ceremony) they use rice, turmeric, and so on (which are also used by any 'upper' castes) but at the same time they also use wool, wool spun into thread, scissors and leaves from different trees. If it is an agrarian family, agricultural tools play a symbolic role in the marriage ceremony.

THE PRIEST AND THE PEOPLE

The priest comes into contact with the Dalitbahujans only on such occasions as marriage and death. And then he comes not to educate them about the spirit that he visualizes as embodied in God; not to talk in a language that people can understand. No mantra he recites is understood by anyone present there—not a word. A priest who treats his subjects as part of his religion must explain the relationship between the divinity and the people, make them conscious about the spirit of the divine. But during that brief contact between them and the priest the people do not feel that he had come to educate them. Each mantra that he murmurs is in a language that none around can understand. The people do not know whether the priest is calling on the divine spirits to bless the couple or curse them. But the end-product of that brief encounter between the priest and the people is that the priest acquires wealth. There are two words that every priest uses at the end of every mantra— the first is 'samarpayaami', and the second, 'swaaha'. The first word means one must give away all at one has, and the second means one ought to eat it all up. Who is it that gets to eat—the priests themselves. Every marriage ends up in a quarrel between the priest and the people over his material demands at the marriage. He takes rice, vegetables, tamarind, dry coconut, cashew nuts and finally *paanbiida* from poor people who have never eaten cashew nuts or paanbiida in their lives. The priest is still not satisfied. He must also be given a specified amount of money. He does not take into account the economic conditions of the marriage party. On the contrary, he demands that their economic conditions must measure up to his demands. In these families on that marriage day the problem is not dowry but *dakshina*. The dakshina operates as *danda* (cane; force). By inviting the priest they do not invite pleasure, but invite a pain—a terrible pain at that.

The people sitting or standing around the marriage pandal might be thin, pale looking and emaciated. Many of them would have been starving for quite some time before the marriage day. Their clothes might have been in tatters for years and years but on that marriage day either by raising loans or by spending what they had saved by pulling paise and paise together, they buy some new clothes for themselves. Even on their 'well-dressed' occasion the priest looks abnormally different from them. His overgrown belly, his unexercised muscles hanging from his bones, his oily skin, his clean-shaven head (the barber can touch him only while shaving and never again) all must be seen to be believed. The Dalitbahujans celebrating the marriage look as if their blood has been siphoned into the priest's body. This can happen not merely because they live in a structure called caste in homogeneous Hinduism. This happens because the priest treats them as the 'outsiders' of his religion. He does not treat them as 'children of that God' in whom he believes. He believes and treats them as outsiders because the audiences of his mantras are his enemies. In his view they are objects from whom dakshina can be extracted. In his view they are the dogs that need to be taught obedience—and a perpetual obedience at that.

In the relationship between the priest and the people there is no spirituality at all. The subjects in this relationship are not treated as those whose 'eyes must be opened to see the light of God' but are treated as those whose eyes have to be plucked out lest they perceive the conspiracy between the man called priest and his God. To put it in simple terms, the relationship between the priest and the people on all such occasions when he comes in contact with them, is the relationship between exploiter and exploited. It is worse than that of a feudal lord and a serf, or a capitalist and a worker.

The feudal lord and the capitalist speak in a language that the serf and the worker can understand. The physical survival of serf's becomes the feudal lord's own interest because their daily alienated labour keeps the exploiter's surplus growing. Between the Hindu priest and the Dalitbahujan masses even that concern is not there. The inhuman relationship that exists between priest and people does not end only in economic exploitation. It has a much deeper social dimension. While keeping the people soulless, spiritless, unrelated in any form to that God in whom the priest has enormous faith, he structures their social behaviour in a very communicable language. While he recites every word of the mantra in an incomprehensible Sanskrit, he tells them what to do and how to satisfy that God in relation to himself. He asks them to produce article after article. He asks them to sit, stand and walk seven steps around that burning fire. They do not know the meaning of all this, even today, despite the Hindutva movement which claims that all Dalitbahujans are Hindus. And yet generation after generation this has continued. The marriage ceremony ends when all who are present touch the feet of the priest: a brazenly shameful act. It is not a voluntary act. It is a subtly manipulated, coercive act. The whole of Dalitbahujan society is coerced to behave in accordance with the wishes of the priest. If anyone revolts against that act of touching his feet, the priest incites the elders standing around, demanding that they mend the ways of such rebellious persons. The incitement is couched in the language of sin and rebellion, described as a sin against God. The elders are made to feel that sense of sin, and are in turn made to force the youth, even if they are rebellious, to mend their ways. The whole community is thus made subservient, timid and fearful.

The married life of the Dalitbahujans is not like that of the Hindu *grihastaas* (householders). The three words that the priests make the Dalitbahujans repeat at the time of the marriage, in a language that they do not understand, *ardheecfia, kaameecha, dharmeecha*— do not mean anything to them in practice. As I said earlier, marriage for the Dalitbahujans is a coming together of a man and a woman for the production of food, goods and commodities and also for the procreation of the human species.

The Hindu religion did not organize its own people to take up collective economic activity. The priest's family and his whole caste never share productive work with the Dalitbahujans. Dalitbahujan married couples can never enjoy a sexual life that is anywhere like the Hindu enjoyment as it is narrated by the Hindu *kama* pandit, Vatsyayana. Let us first discuss our people's relation to *artha* (economy). A great majority of the Dalitbahujans live in small hutments in villages and in the urban slums. It is the life in rural India that is the root of the community's culture and also its economy.

PRODUCTION

A Dalitbahujan couple rises every morning at *koodikuuta* (cockcrow). The man enters directly into his agrarian tasks, the woman begins immediately on her household activities. Bath and prayer have no place in their lives at that juncture. The man has to feed his cattle and clean the cattleshed. A Kurumaa man hardly sleeps at home. Wherever the herd of sheep sleeps, that is his living place. Early in the morning he gets up, separates his own sheep from the general herd. Next, he releases the younger ones from the *podhi* (an enclosure where the young sheep are kept) and takes them to their mother to be suckled. Then they examine the diseased cattle or sheep and apply medicines. A Goudaa gets up and straightaway puts on his toddy-climbing clothes and goes to the toddy tree rows. He knows his toddy trees by name as the shepherd knows his sheep or goats by name and as the peasants know their cows, bulls and buffaloes by name. The Goudaa climbs his first tree at sunrise. He is the one who gets to see the beauty of nature at sunrise from the tallest tree. Poised at the top, he skilfully chooses the point at which he makes the first cut to his *gela* (a projection on the toddy tree from where the toddy is tapped). It is not the time now to take the toddy that has accumulated in the *kallumuntha* (a small pot in which the toddy is tapped). It is the time to check that the toddy drops flow from the gela without impediment. The Malaas or Maadigaas rise from their beds and begin either to clean and cure skins or prepare the leather for shoe-making. In the majority of cases, they then go to their master's fields to cut the crop or to bundle it up.

In these families what they must do every morning is not decided by them but by their masters. The women in these families get up and go to the master's cattlesheds to clean them, or to sweep the surroundings of the master's houses—but certainly not to sweep the inside of the house. They rush back home only to find empty cooking pots waiting to be washed, hungry children waiting for some food. They do not have time to think about God or prayer. After that the women cook some *ambali* (a sort of porridge), the food of the poor where even the one curry as it is made in a Kurumaa or a Goudaa house does not exist. Hence they cook some liquid stuff to swallow. The woman must rush because they must reach the working point in the fields much before the dawn breaks. All Dalitbahujan men and women must do this. Their work never starts with a morning prayer or a cold water bath. The *surya-vandanam* (morning prayer) that the Hindu does never finds a place in their day's timetable.

A Hindu—a Brahmin, Baniya or Kshatriya—on the other hand, gets up to take a cold water bath and then still clad in wet clothes picks up his book—the Gita—and begins to relate to God. He or she asks God for the day's food, the day's *gyana* (knowledge) and the day's *sheela* (character). God for them is a stud-bull that can produce everything. All difficult and delicate tasks can be taken care of by him. The priest, therefore, leaves everything to him.

As a Telugu poet has said, in Hindu consciousness, God sits in the heart and makes it run, he sits in the flower and structures the colours in it, he sits in the sky and makes it rain. He makes streams flow and the mountains grow. He changes the seas. A Hindu relates in prayer and meditation to this God and thereafter he changes from the *tadivastram* (wet cloth) to a *pattuvastram* (silk cloth) which, of course, no Dalitbahujan can ever dream of wearing.

COOKING

A Dalitbahujan woman gets up from her bed and picks up her water pot, fetches water for cooking, sweeps the house and *waakili* (the open place in front of the house), cleans the cattleshed (if there is one), lights the hearth, pours out the kuraadu water, and puts on the cooking pot. She then struggles hard to light the hearth that cooks the day's food. Unlike the Hindu woman, she does not think about God before entering the kitchen, and does not think about maintaining the purity of madi. For a Hindu woman, this is a precondition before she can make the *palahaaram* (breakfast). For a Dalitbahujan woman cooking is a mundane activity, meant to feed the human body and keep it going, whereas for a Hindu, God is central even to the kitchen. A Dalitbahujan woman cooks some rice or jawar and a curry. If there is some buttermilk to add to it that day, it goes down better. The notion of God and the notion of religion do not figure in the cooking. A Hindu woman's cooking takes place primarily in the name of God. There is palahaaram, *payaasam* (sweet rice), a dozen curries, *daddoojanam* (curd rice fried in oil), *pulihoora* (sour rice), *saambaar* (dal and tamarind mixture), *rasam* (vegetable liquid), with *perugannam* (curd rice) to end the eating process. All these are prepared with care and caution as food that is offered to God. But where does the concept of *prasaadam* (food offered to God) exist in our homes? The number of items of that godly food can be seen in any modern 'Brahmin' hotel that serves a *taalibhoojanam* (plate meal). It is the God's duty to digest all these and also look after the health of the eaters. God must save them from overeating and from the diseases caused by the fatty food. It is for this reason that all cooking activity begins with prayer, and eating activity begins with prayer. The relationship between God and priest here becomes a friendly relationship between God and glutton. But the situation in the Dalitbahujan castes is totally different.

As soon as the cooking activity of a Dalitbahujan woman is over, she feeds the children, swallows some food to satisfy the burning hunger in her stomach, packs some food for her husband and leaves for the field. The furrowing of lands, seeding and watering— all these are collective activities of both woman and man. It is not that the patriarchal 'strong' and 'weak' relations do not operate even in the field in these castes. They do, but they operate at a mundane level. Power relations between men and women are not 'sacred' and therefore are less manipulative. The divine stories do not structure them into an ideology that works on the human plane as male control over the female. To that extent this is a less complicated and less oppressive relationship than the relationship between man and woman among the Hindus.

FEMALE AND MALE DOMAINS

In Kurumaa, Gollaa, Goudaa, Maalaa, or Maadigaa and other castes, the man does the work that is defined as 'male' work and the woman does the work that is defined as 'female' work. For example, in Kurumaa families going along with sheep, herding them, cutting the wool, milking the animals, are all male tasks. The women make the thread out of wool and attend to many other tasks that convert wool into blankets. By the time the crop comes into their hands, by the time the sheep delivers, by the time toddy is brought down, by the time the shoes are ready in these communities, both man and woman can claim that both of them have contributed to its making—and for the professions' making itself. For the Hindu woman on the other hand, cooking, maintaining the house, procreating are all done in the name of God and man. They cannot claim to be contributors to their respective professions—whether of priesthood or of business. Their existence is subsumed into their husbands' existence.

In this society, the man is abnormally strong and the woman is abnormally weak. For example, a peasant woman can at times move out of her traditional role of seeding and weeding to plough the land: a Kurumaa woman can become a sheep-breeder in the absence of the man. A Brahmin woman, however, can never become a priest. A Dalitbahujan woman within her caste/class existence is very much a political being, a social being and an economic being. Whereas, a Brahmin woman is not. The Dalitbahujan castes have a philosophy in performing productive work which is distinctly different from the Hindu's philosophy. It is not a divine philosophy. It is a mundane, human philosophy. It does not belong to the 'other world' and 'other life' but deals with this world. Its everyday life belongs to the present *janma* (life). This philosophy is taught right from our childhood, and it seeps into the making of our beings. Our whole philosophy is expressed in one sentence which can be understood, not only by these communities but also by the Brahmins and the Baniyas. But they do not want to take it seriously. In fact they do not even want to hear it. For them it is the unmentionable; that which should not be spoken or heard because their own philosophy is couched in divine terms and it is quite the opposite of Dalitbahujan philosophy. There is a simple sentence that repeatedly expresses the philosophy of Dalitbahujans. That simple sentence is *rekkaaditeegaani bukkaadadu* ('unless the hand works the mouth cannot eat'). This philosophical sentence is not speaking in terms of the hand that holds the bow and arrow as Rama did, or the hand that holds the *chakram* as Vishnu and Krishna did. It speaks about the hand that holds the plough to furrow the land and the hand that holds the seeds to seed those furrows and the hand that ensures that the plants grow out of those furrows and nurses them till they yield fruits.

Do these toiling people know that the Bhagavad Gita, one of the Hindu texts, has a philosophy which is the exact opposite? Do they know that the text also speaks its philosophy in one poetic stanza, but what is that philosophical stanza? 'You have the right to work but not to the fruits.' I too would not have understood the meaning of this stanza if a foreigner had not translated the Gita into English. It is our people's misfortune that the priest who extract dakshina from them on every occasion that he visits them, never tells them about this sentence contained in the philosophy of the Other. It establishes an ideology which says that our masses must work, but they must not aspire to enjoy the fruits of that work. Where ought those fruits to go? The Hindu system established a network of institutions to siphon the fruits of people's work into Hindu families who treat the work as mean and dirty. Apart from the institution of priests that extracts the fruits of Dalitbahujan work without even letting the masses come in touch with the divine spirit, there is that institution of *vaisya vyaapaaram* (Baniya business) that must be undertaken only by the Baniyas. It is through this institution of vaisya vyaapaaram that the labour of the Dalitbahujans gets exploited. How does this vyapaaram take place?

BANIYA ECONOMY

In every village there are a small number of Baniya families. They are known as *koomaties* or *shahukars*. In the Baniya families, ritualistic formations are more or less like those of the Brahmin families. These families are distinctly different from our families. In spiritual terms the Baniyas relate to the Brahmins. The formation of the consciousness of their children is absolutely identical—the stories that they are told, the life-styles that they have to acquire, are very similar to those of a Brahmin child. A Baniya male child like a Brahmin male child has to undergo an upanayana and a Baniya girl has to learn to cook as many items as a Brahmin child, and that too in madi purity. In their narratives the dominant story is that of Kubeera, who is a God who eats a lot, who is a plunderer and a stingy preserver of wealth. After marriage—child marriage is much prevalent in these families—a Baniya is supposed to establish a business, the art of which is taught right from childhood.

A Baniya is a seated divine-intellectual whose contact with people is daily and hourly. His house must be centrally located so that masses can easily come and go; in that house he establishes a structured shop which provides the mechanism for buying and selling. He buys grain, pulses, vegetables, everything that the masses produce, and he sells them clothes, oil, spices and also grain and pulses. In other words he is a collector and a distributor of goods, grain, pulses, salt, oil, and so on. Unlike the priest he prefers to meet the Dalitbahujan sellers and buyers one by one—not in groups—because he has to communicate to them in a language they can understand. He cannot speak in Sanskrit as the priest does for the simple reason that the market transactions must take place in a language that the people can understand. His aim is that people—one by one—should be manipulated in a language of communication; yet he must also ensure that the manipulation should not be apparent to the collective consciousness of the masses.

In physical terms the Baniya is a heavy and hefty person with a pot belly and with unexercised hanging muscles. He has a white thread hanging around his body and a *naamam* (a three-line white tilak) on his forehead. Physically he is distinctly different from his customers. They are frail and weak-bodied. The masses are unclad for the simple reason that they do not have clothes for themselves. The Baniya shahukar is also semi-naked because he must appear to be divine. Whatever he wears on his semi-naked body is worth thousands of rupees. He would have a golden chain around his neck and would be wearing a pattuvastram.

A Baniya woman is distinctly different from the whole mass of village women as much as the Brahmin woman is. But at the same time a Brahmin woman is different from a Baniya woman in two ways. While a Brahmin woman is an expert only in divine cooking, the Baniya woman is a part of the home-centred business. She establishes a skilful rapport with the Dalitbahujan womenfolk to lure them into their own shop. She deals with them one by one so that her manipulations are not understood by the masses and so that they never become a part of mass consciousness. She is as skilful a manipulator of female customers as her husband is of male customers. The lies they tell, the deceitful mechanisms that they evolve, over a period of time, establishes a particular system of Hindu market. The establishment of Hindu market relations have several specific forms. A non-Hindu (feudal or capitalist) market, particularly in the West, is a standardized market. A businessman or a businesswoman does not have to tell lies about the purchase price, and a lie will not become part of the surplus. But a Hindu Baniya market presupposes a lie to be part of its sacred form as well as its business culture. A Baniya is said to be within his Hindu morality—in spite of the fact that he misleads his customers and tells lies about his margins of profit. He will retain his Hindu morality even if he underweighs while selling and overweighs while buying. He will be within his Hindu morality even if he over-rates the quality of the commodity he sells, or under-rates the quality while buying. A Baniya is extremely Hinduistic. Even the prices of commodities or grain and pulses change based on the caste of the customer. For example, for the same grain a Maadigaa gets paid less than a Reddy gets. While buying from the Baniya, the lower the caste of the customer, the higher would be the price, and while selling it would be the opposite. In any village market, all roads lead to one place—the shahukar's shop.

This does not mean that specific caste-based producers do not have their own specific markets. They do have these. For example, there are some caste-related markets where the buyers and sellers operate outside the Hindu Baniya market. In most parts of India the Baniya refuses to buy anything that is a non-Hindu commodity. Selling and buying cattle and beef is non-Hindu; selling and buying sheep and mutton is non-Hindu; selling and buying fish is non-Hindu; selling and buying toddy is non-Hindu; and finally, selling and buying leather-related commodities is non-Hindu. Thus the chappal, a *baareda* (a leather belt that is hung around the neck of a bull) and a *vaarena* (leather thongs) are non-Hindu commodities, and the selling and buying of these are part of the work of Dalitbahujan markets. So these markets are handled by individuals coming from Dalitbahujan castes, Muslims or Christians. These markets operate outside the principle of divinity—they are 'secular' markets. As the sacred ethos is absent here, the quotations, and so on, are straightforward, the market terms are communicable.

Sometimes the seller sympathizes with the buyer if his/her economic condition is known to him/her. Payment becomes possible in instalments. In other words socially, economically and philosophically the sellers and buyers relate to each other in these non-Hindu markets. This does not mean the influence of Baniya market principles is totally invisible here. The shahukar sets an example even for these market relations. But the significant difference lies in the way people relate to each other socially and philosophically. Perhaps, this could be one of the reasons why the non-Hindu, Dalitbahujan market dealers do not become visibly rich. His/her life-style rarely becomes significantly different from those of the masses.

MAN AND WOMAN RELATIONS

Are the man-woman relations of Dalitbahujan families and Hindu families the same? In my view there is a categorical difference. The marital life of every couple is based on the couple's respective childhood formations. But the significant difference between Dalitbahujans and Hindus in this context begins with an absolutely opposite approach to the concept of *kama* (sexual love). In both kinds of families, at the time of marriage the priest talks about *kaameecha.* For a Dalitbahujan couple and a Brahmin or a Baniya couple, the concept may appear to be strange in the beginning. There is an essential difference also in the practical and philosophical points of view. Indeed there is a paradox in the experiences and education of persons born in these two families. The Dalitbahujan couple would have heard about sexual desire from the experiences of parents, relations and friends. But in the narratives of Dalitbahujan Gods and Goddesses descriptions of kama are totally absent. They know nothing about the personal lives of Pochamma, Maisamma, Maramma, Potaraju, Malliah, and others. Each one of these Goddesses and Gods has a narrative. Even young people relate to these Goddesses and Gods but nowhere in those narratives does love appear as desire. The Brahmin-Baniyas impose a ban on sexual discourse at the human plane. The strict restriction imposed on women's mobility cuts down the interaction between men and women. It also cuts down the interaction between 'upper' caste and Dalitbahujan women. So the pleasures missing in the social plane in day-to-day living are sought to be derived from divine sexual experiences. To understand such paradoxes one should understand the sexuality of the Hindu Goddesses and Gods.

The stories of Hindu Gods and Goddesses are full of descriptions of sexual encounters. The most powerful narrative exists in the form of Goddess and God relations among Hindu men and women. Krishna and Radha, Varudhini and Pravarakya, Shankara and Parvathi are well-known examples. But the most powerful story is that of Radha and Krishna. The most restrictive brahminical families not only permit young girls to worship Krishna who is a patriarchal sexist God but also to love him; a girl can invite him to bestow his love on her. He is carved into all sorts of poses and postures, colours and costumes. Many Hindu texts, the Bhagavad Gita is an exception, are full of such narratives. The most powerful text that influences Hindu thought in terms of man-woman relations is Vatsyayana's *Kamasutra.* But for the leisure available at the disposal of brahminical families and the atmosphere in which they live, sixty-four forms of sexual expression could not have been possible. This life was projected as divine and hence even the Hindu temples become the places where Vatsyayana's sixty-four forms are part of the sculpture.

The man-woman relationship in Dalitbahujan families is markedly different. The sexual relationship has never been projected into an art form. This does not mean they do not sing songs based on love stories. They sing the love stories of people around them. The narrative is basically secular. Yet another big difference between the family life of the Hindus and the Dalitbahujan castes is that the Hindus make sex a leisure-bound divine activity whereas among the Dalitbahujans, family life is a part of production. For them leisure and holiday are unknown. In certain castes interaction between wife and husband is often momentary. For example, in Kurumaa families during the day, the man would go into forests along with the sheep or the goats and in the night he would usually sleep with the herd. The woman would perform all the family tasks. She would do the purchasing, look after the children. If there were no wool-related work, she would take on agrarian tasks in order to add to the income. In all those operations she would deal with civil society alone. Thus in those families the whole life-process gives little scope for divinity and pleasure. The man would meet his wife sometimes near midnight and go back to his herd.

In other words, man-woman relations among Dalitbahujans do not go beyond 'natural' relationships. For those who have not come in touch with letters, for those whose spiritual wisdom is primitive but natural because it has not acquired the character of manipulation and exploitation, the human touch is still retained. In these societies, hegemonic relations in the forms that are visible among the Hindus are absent. Here even sexual intercourse is an organic need of the body but not a pleasure of the heart. This undefined love retains its naturalness among the Dalitbahujans. Among the Hindus the man-woman relationship is conditioned by manipulation and deceptivity. Dalitbahujan relationships on the other hand are based on openness.

A consciousness that gives more importance to nature than to sacred beings is always stronger. It is a consciousness that constructs its own kind of character. This character is different from that moulded by the fear of external agencies. The Dalitbahujans of India are the only people on the globe who, while living in a civil society, have lived outside the defined structures of all religions. Take, for example, their marriage contract. It is basically a human contract. It is governed by the rights guaranteed to women within the framework of the broad system of patriarchy. A situation of disrespect to each other's rights can result in breaking that contract and will result in divorce. If after divorce the woman or the man comes across another possible partner, either by way of parental arrangement or because of her/his own initiative, such individuals have the right to enter into another contract. Because of these inherently assured rights, a wife does not have to treat her husband as a God. A Dalitbahujan woman does not have to perform *padapuja* (worshipping the husband's feet) to her husband either in the morning or in the evening. She does not have to address her husband in the way she would address a superior. In a situation of dispute, word in response to word, and abuse for abuse is the socially visible norm. Patriarchy as a system does exist among Dalitbahujans, yet in this sense it is considerably more democratic.

A Dalitbahujan couple may also aspire for a son but for entirely different reasons as compared to the Hindus. As I said earlier, among the Dalitbahujans the son is not a divine gift to take the father to heaven. A son in their view is a relatively more productive force. This view itself is based on an unscientific understanding, which is governed by human limitations and also conditioned by the process of their development. The Dalitbahujan personality hangs between materialism and spiritualism, whereas the Hindu personality is made out of decadent spiritualism. In this decadent spiritualism, marriage, market, manhood and womanhood are structured in irrational forms. Hindu values mould individuals who cannot tolerate the spiritual equality of others. In its day-to-day operations a Hindu family does not run on a human plane. It is a divinely-animated collective affair. It has established institutional structures that do not reflect a spiritual system that can draw more and more human beings into it. Dalitbahujan spiritualism on the contrary is nonreligious but humane.

If Hinduism were to establish, even within the spiritual domain, an attractive relationship of humanity, perhaps Hinduism would have become a universal religion earlier than Buddhism, Christianity or Islam. The family structure that it established, instead of attracting fellow human beings, repelled them. It established a market system that created structures that sucked the energy of Dalitbahujan masses who were denied even that notional right to swarga. The Hindus are the only people who converted even spirituality and the promise of redemption in the other world into the private property of only Brahmins, Vaisyas and Kshatriyas. Unfortunately, the 'Sudra upper castes' (like Reddies, Kammas, Velamas in Andhra Pradesh; Marathas, Patels, Jats, Rajputs, Bhumihars in North India) who are emerging slowly as neo-Kshatriyas are moving into the fold of Hindutva both physically and mentally.

CHAPTER 3

The Emergence of Neo-Kshatriyas and the Reorganization of Power Relations

Every village is a political power centre. Political power in a village community operates both at the micro-level and the macro-level. However, our consciousnesses are formed in such a way that many of the operations of power become invisible. In the earlier chapters, I have tried to show how, at every stage in the human life cycle— childhood formation, man-woman relations, family making—as well as in market relations, the Dalitbahujan and the Hindu approaches to life are totally different. This difference has serious socioeconomic implications for the political formations of Dalitbahujans.

CASTE AND POWER

The traditional Hindu understanding is that political power is to be held only by Kshatriyas and that Brahmins are to assist them in ministerial positions. But this is an inadequate understanding. Power relations cannot be discussed merely in terms of institutions that relate to the state. The Dalitbahujans live very much within a certain framework of power relations. First and foremost the caste system itself sets up a certain type of power relations. The Maalaas and the Maadigaas, right from childhood, are trained more to obey and to listen than to command and to speak. Starting from this early age one learns to listen and to obey or to speak and to command depending on the status of one's caste. The lower the caste of the person, the higher will be the level of obedience, and the higher the caste of the person, the stronger will be the motivation to speak and to command. Take, for example, the Kurumaa caste, which is a middle-rung caste. Kurumaas can command Maalaas, Maadigaas, Chakaalies, Mangalies. Irrespective of their ages, people coming from the so-called higher castes can address the Dalitbahujan castes in a demeaning manner (a male person is addressed as *are* and a female person is addressed as *yende, yevvative*). This itself establishes certain power relations. The Kurumaas have to behave differently in the presence of persons belonging to 'higher' castes. Castes higher than the Kurumaas, beginning with the Kapuus, think that they have a right to humiliate and insult Dalitbahujan men and women.

The power relations between castes are so structured that the self-respect which is of critical importance in developing the personality of Dalitbahujan women/men is mutilated. In all South Indian villages (this may be true of North India too), the Kshatriya caste which handled the institution of state power has become dormant and a neo-Kshatriya force from the 'Sudra upper' castes have began to emerge. In Andhra Pradesh, for example, the Reddies, Velamas and Kammas are increasingly coming to believe not only that they form a part of the Hindu religion but also that they are castes who have the right to insult others. In ritual terms they are not *dwijas,* or twice-born, but today in political terms they are attempting to play the role of the classical Kshatriyas by establishing their hegemony in all structures in which power operates.

NEO-KSHATRIYA CONSCIOUSNESS

The neo-Kshatriyas believe that they are part of Hindu spirituality. They are becoming patrons of Hindutva. While the Brahmin-Baniyas manipulate our consciousness in spiritual and economic domains, the neo-Kshatriyas think that by stepping into the shoes of the 'classical' Kshatriyas they can manipulate power relations at various levels. Hinduism believes in the theory of co-optation and exclusion. The Brahmin-Baniyas are slowly co-opting the neo-Kshatriyas and excluding the castes below them. The surest way of structuring power relations and maintaining hegemony is by acquiring control of cultivable land and by systematically excluding the Other from controlling the land and land-related means of production. The neo-Kshatriyas have an added advantage in this as they are not yet completely alienated from the agrarian production process and hence are culturally and knowledge-wise rooted in agrarian arts and agrarian science. There are some poor and semi-poor families who in caste terms belong to neo-Kshatriya groups such as the Reddies; yet by the very placement of their class they are in day-to-day touch with Dalitbahujans.

These families function as connecting links between the Brahmin-Baniyas and the lower castes. This is how the political hegemony of the neo-Kshatriyas gets maintained on an hourly and daily basis. The neo-Kshatriyas meet persons belonging to the Dalitbahujan castes in their fields and at their houses every day. This process of constant interaction ensures that unequal relations are perpetuated. The Brahmin-Baniyas on the other hand interact with Dalitbahujans on far fewer occasions. Brahminism would have weakened substantially as a result of the spreading of modernity into the villages but for the emergence of the neo-Kshatriya cultural forms. Thus, the neo-Kshatriyas have become the saviours of Brahminism. However, they are also operating as a rootless social force. They are reluctant to own up to the culture of Pochamma and Maisamma in which they are actually rooted; at the same time they are rebuffed by Brahminism which does not want to extend to them the status of the dwija castes. Despite this they continue aggressively to identify themselves with Brahminism and with the Hindutva that it is producing in order to subvert democratic relations in the political and economic structures that are basically the by-products of Dalitbahujan socio-political subsystems.

In fact, the neo-Kshatriya castes are attempting to acquire for themselves a new cultural status. Their male children are brought up in an artificial heritage of martial culture. We find this in their names to which suffixes like Reddy, Rao, Patel and Singh are increasingly added. The stress in these families is on acquiring economic and political power. In keeping with this ambiguity their women are being pushed into practicing neo-*madi* (purity rituals in the form of wet clothing after bathing) cultural forms. A neo-Kshatriya wife addresses the husband using the respectful form of 'you', in the plural, while the husband addresses the wife not only in singular but in the demeaning forms (yende, *yeme)*. Distancing themselves from actual work in the fields and manipulating 'lower' caste labour into doing all the hard work are some of the new arts being taught to their men and women. Like the Brahmin-Baniyas, they are attempting to teach their female children to be docile and submissive sexual objects. These children are being trained to cook multi-itemed vegetarian and non-vegetarian meals. The notion of the sacred is beginning to enter into their cooking and eating habits. Particularly among women, a daily puja is becoming part of their consciousness.

The neo-Kshatriya ambition is not to dalitize or democratize human relations, but to brahminize them. If they were to dalitize their culture, their work ethic would have been different. They would not have put an end to their interaction with the productive fields. This section of society understands the link between land and political power. So, right from childhood, neo-Kshatriya children are taught to acquire both by adopting any means. In this respect brahminical Kautilyanism comes handy to them. Their domination is evident in every aspect of day-to-day life, even in civil society. In one sense they have made politics and power obvious aspects of life. Yet because of their roots in agriculture and their ambiguous, non-dwija spiritual status, they hang between democracy and dictatorship as their political form.

DALITBAHUJAN PATRIARCHAL DEMOCRACY

Among the Dalitbahujans political relations within the family or community setting are basically democratic. In terms of the parent-children relationship, politics operates in what might be termed a 'patriarchal democracy'. A Dalitbahujan household is not essentially 'private'. In fact the notion of private does not exist in Dalitbahujan consciousness. Among these castes the house is very much a social unit. This is an accepted norm. Wife-beating is a patriarchal practice that exists among all castes. Dalitbahujans are not exempt from this vice. But the beaten-up wife has a right to make the attack public by shouting, abusing the husband and, if possible, by beating the husband in return. The women and the men in the community both have the right to interfere, arbitrate and take the quarrel to the caste panchayats.

The caste panchayat pertaining to man-woman problems, inter-family or intra-family disputes takes place in the open. Everyone who is present has a right to be involved in evolving a judgement. Dalitbahujan law does not emerge from authority; it arises out of the community. The openness with which it functions itself works as a check against injustice. Since the notion of 'private' does not exist, every cause and consequence is debated. This does not mean that violence doesn't take place. But when brutality takes place, the positive aspects of Dalitbahujan law prevail and public outrage becomes an instrument.

One of the important mechanisms of this public outrage is found in the congress of women's deliberations popularly known as *Ammalakkala Muchchatlu* (the deliberations of the mothers and sisters). These deliberations are open. They are political and juridical in nature and evolve a feminine consensus for resolving problems. A careful observation of the Dalitbahujan panchayat juridical system and the Ammalakkala Muchchatlu indicates that the law of the Dalitbahujans does not distinguish between public and private. Its juridical philosophy itself does not believe in the notion of private. Perhaps this is rooted into the Dalitbahujan existence itself. The Ammalakkala congresses engage in constant debates. These debates take place in a variety of locations and at various times. They take place in the mornings and evenings, inside the village as well as in the fields. In addition, these discussions take on an inter-caste nature. The very mode of Dalitbahujan existence makes the notion of 'private' impossible, indeed unthinkable. This is true not only of the notion 'private', the notion 'personal' also does not exist. Every personal relationship among the Dalitbahujans is both social and political. Here human bonds are structured in terms of 'we' but not 'I'. Even if the concept 'I' exists, it does not have the same meaning among the 'lower' castes as it has among the 'upper' castes. The former refer to their mother as 'our mother', to the house as 'our house', to the fields as 'our fields'. The individual here is a part of a collective. And that collective is both social and political. The caste community does not provide space for the autonomy of the individual. The individual is always a part of the larger collective and the collective functions in an open way.

For the Dalitbahujans individualism is an expression of negative 'will'. There is nothing like 'mine'. Everything is 'ours'. If a person expresses his negative will by individualizing anything as personal, the collective consciousness expresses itself and brings that individual back into the collective fold. Every home and caste operation is a commune in itself. This commune is under-developed no doubt. In terms of consciousness we might say that most of the Dalitbahujan castes keep struggling between the notions of private property and communal property. Higher up in the caste hierarchy the notion of private property becomes greater. For example, the notion of private property is minimal among Maadigaas and Maalaas. Preserving for the next day, for the next month and for the next year has not yet become part of the consciousness of these Scheduled Castes. By and large the Scheduled Castes have retained the tribal notion of property as 'public' for thousands of years. Whatever the Dalitbahujans procure—a dead cow or bull—or when they cut a living sheep or goat, they divide it equally among themselves. In thousands of caste wadaas, particularly, Scheduled Caste wadaas, equal distribution takes place in the form of *poogulu* or *kuppalu* or *paallu* (if it is mutton or beef dividing it into as many equal shares as the number of families; or if it is grain, again equal shares). Those who work more, fetching cattle or sheep, do not get more than the others. Someone may have worked more on that occasion, but the share he/she gets is equal.

In the post-colonial period, the government has been giving these castes something in order that they might begin acquiring 'assets' (of course, what is given is very little). But even those assets within a short time are converted into public assets. The state agencies, and also the Indian 'upper' castes, have been criticizing the culture of dispossession among the Scheduled Castes as 'spendthrift'. These groups speak of the latter as 'lazy fellows'. An incessant discourse among the so-called upper castes, often expounded in abusive language is that these 'lower caste bastards' should not be given anything as they do not know how to retain or invest it. But the 'upper' caste criticism is absolutely wrong. The Dalitbahujan culture that India has is a remarkable legacy. The Dalitbahujans have never believed that power is embodied in property. The 'upper' caste condemnation, that the Scheduled Castes are unworthy of possessing property, is actually turning Dalitbahujan philosophy upside down. A community that has lived for thousands of years with no notion of private property will quickly dispossess themselves of it, even if it is given to them in charity or by 'welfarism'. The very notion of private property goes against its philosophy. It is not the weakness of a people but their strength. Actually this is where the future of India lies.

BRAHMINICAL PATRIARCHY

Beginning with the neo-Kshatriyas, as you move upwards in the caste hierarchy, the notions of power, property, private, public and personal changes greatly. The neo-Kshatriyas have slowly given up their caste panchayats. Similarly, hierarchy is slowly entering their homes. As their homes move from the secular to the spiritual domain, their notion of power revolves around divinity, and human beings begin to look like nonentities. The homes of neo-Kshatriyas are split between a divine and a brahminized femininity and an aggrandized masculine power structure which appears at times divine and at times secular. Neo-Kshatriya masculine power hobnobs with Brahminism as it is perfectly well-suited to the philosophy of casteism. At the same time, however, it wants to displace the Brahmins and the Baniyas physically from the hegemonic locations of political power and of the market.

In the post-1947 period, in the all-India context, the Brahmins and the Baniyas have acquired hegemony both in politics and in business. Alongside this development there emerged an all-India neo-Kshatriya social base which is ideologically aligned with the Brahmin-Baniyas. In a situation that witnessed the total decline of classical Kshatriyas, the neo-Kshatriyas found enormous economic and political space for themselves. This is one of the reasons why in the context of the 1990 post-Mandal assertions of Dalitbahujan castes, the neo-Kshatriyas found an entrenched place in Hindutva. The Brahmin-Baniyas also felt that an ally who has an agrarian base and does not feel totally alienated from brahminical spirituality is essential to sustain its politico-economic and spiritual power.

The alliance of Brahmin-Baniya and neo-Kshatriya is being projected as a sort of modernity of India. This Hinduized modernity is historically a negative development. It is an anti-thesis of Dalitbahujan assertion. In fact, post-colonial Hindutva is a brahminical modernity which works strategically in the interest of Brahmin, Baniya and neo-Kshatriya forces. Its historical aim is to subvert the political assertion of the Dalitbahujan castes which form the democratic and secular social base of India. If the Brahmin-Baniya and neo-Kshatriya combine operates in the secular domain, these democratic forces will not be able to acquire or sustain power. Hence the 'upper' caste combine has reason to mix spiritualism and political power. The blend of spiritualism and political power is very much rooted in their casteized patriarchal authoritarianism. Brahminical authoritarianism can express itself in neo-fascist forms, while also attempting to establish control over the institutions of state and civil society by bringing into existence all kinds of classical brahminical notions of life itself.

In terms of power relations, Brahmin families are anti-democratic. As mentioned earlier, Brahminism's undemocratic system is rooted in its notion of the spiritual and the divine. To begin with, its notion of Gods and Goddesses and the relations between these notional Gods and Goddesses are shaped in patriarchal authoritarianism. This is very clear from the notional relationship that exists between Brahma and Saraswathi, Vishnu and Lakshmi, and Shiva and Parvathi and also the rest of the Gods and the Goddesses. The Hindu Gods and Goddesses are made in the cultural image of Brahmins.

A Brahmin family is a reflection of these notions of patriarchal authoritarianism. The male patriarch establishes his authority over the entire family—particularly over the women, not because he possesses any special ability, but by creating and constantly reinforcing the consciousness of patriarchal authoritarianism in terms of spirituality. The manipulation of the consciousness of the family members takes place in terms of projecting the patriarchal Gods' all-powerfulness. This power is demonstrated not in terms of the Gods' ability to sacrifice, but in terms of their power to manipulate, defeat and kill. The hierarchy of the family is effected in accordance with the desire of these patriarchal Gods. Women and children have to function in accordance with the dictates of the father, who himself is not a producer, only a conduit of spiritual communication. This is the most negative relationship that Hindu Brahminism has propounded and established. It has negated production and highlighted spirituality. Its supreme task is communication with an abstract spirit. This spirit may not even be addressed by the Others in their respective languages. Brahminism not only excludes masses but delegitimizes their languages.

In other words, brahminical patriarchy operates by conditioning two different kinds of mentalities. On the one hand, it creates a mind that can control, manipulate and finally structure: the male mind. On the other hand, it forms a mind that can be manipulated, controlled and structured: the female mind. It does not provide any scope for questioning, debate and discourse. Its history is a history of recitation of that divine word. The Brahmin mind—male and female—is prohibited from interacting with nature or with production tools, indeed with any of the forces of production. Human beings are not supposed to relate to nature and to other human beings, they must relate only to the 'other world'. This is a negation of the very humanity of the human being. Hindu human beings further negate that negation by taking possession of the resulting spirituality as their own property—spirituality becomes the property of the Brahmin. Thus, male Brahmins negate women in their own families and negate Dalitbahujans in the larger society.

This is the reason why brahminical women have to survive as sexual objects or as subjects who only cook and serve. Their 'will' is completely subsumed into the 'Being' of man. They have no right even to become priests. In Hinduism God is private, prayer is private, family is private and wife and children are personal. The Baniyas operate on similar principles in business. Their families being absolutely brahminical and patriarchal, they apply the principle of 'manipulating the mind' to control business and the market perpetually. Here again personal and private are two conditioning factors. Business is private as much as priesthood is. If one is the private property of Brahmins, the other is the private property of Baniyas. Operating in the same ideological domain, classical Kshatriyas structured political power as their private property.

Classical Kshatriyas continued to operate with the principle of divine patriarchy and extended its structures to political power, martial arts, administration and adjudication. In addition, everything related to power was structured in such a manner that it would operate within the sphere of private property. A Brahmin can exercise politico-spiritual power and a Baniya can operate economic power, but no Dalitbahujan can ever operate either form of power. This was because all castes higher than the one that handles an institution automatically have the right to power in that institution. Essentially, however, political power was the domain of the Kshatriyas. The Brahmins have violated this Hindu notion of power during the post-colonial period and monopolized the running of political and administrative institutions by systematically displacing classical Kshatriyas. They have also entered the Baniya domain in a big way. But at the same time the most embourgeoized temple property and priesthood are retained strictly under Brahmin control. Thus when compared to the classical authoritarian position of Brahmins before Muslim invasions and colonial rule, modern, post-colonial authority of the Brahmins has become all the more pervasive. This development has every potential to negate secular modernity and secular socialism in India. This is because a secular modernity and secular socialism can be arrived at only by extending 'lower' caste notions of what is public and what is political. The contrast becomes more obvious if we examine the other patriarchy that exists side by side with brahminical patriarchy.

COMPARISON

Dalitbahujan patriarchy is completely antithetical to brahminical patriarchy. Here too the notion of man being superior and woman being inferior does exist. But when compared to brahminical patriarchy there is a great difference. Within Dalitbahujan patriarchy woman is an agent of both production and reproduction. The domains of man and woman are not completely bifurcated at home and in the field. A man does the cooking while the woman goes to work in the field and the woman does the man's work when the man is away. While cooking or doing agrarian tasks or while performing caste occupational operations there are no gender restrictions in belief or practice. In these spheres specializations are not gender-specific. A Maalaa or Maadigaa woman is as much an expert in leather-based productive tasks as a Maalaa or Maadigaa man is. A Chakaali woman is as much an expert washerwoman as a Chakaali man. A Kurumaa or a Gollaa woman can care for sheep just as a Kurumaa or a Gollaa man can. In these castes knowledge or skills do not function in closely-guarded separate compartments. The man observes the woman's work, the woman observes the man's work. Neither notional nor physical structures are erected between the domains of the sexes.

It is true that women in the Dalitbahujan castes too have lost political control over their children who are being projected as the property of men. But at the same time, the fact is that the woman is a political being at home, in the Ammalakkala deliberations, and in the field congregations. Consequently the Dalitbahujan woman still enjoys an autonomous social status and retains considerable control over her children. One can find hundreds and thousands of cases where the divorced woman is given the authority to take her children along with her. In several Dalitbahujan castes the woman is the main social agent who oversees the interactions of the family in civil society. She trains the children, shapes them as she wants. This does not mean the Dalitbahujan women and the female political society that they create are free from internalized patriarchal values. They are not. Women teach their female children the morality of being 'women' and the male children the way to be 'men' which in concrete reality goes in the interest of men. But what is important is that when compared to the Brahmins, the Baniyas and the Neo-Kshatriyas the man-woman relations among the Dalitbahujans are far more democratic. Thus they can envisage rebellion and attempt to break the shackles of patriarchy far more easily than 'upper' caste women ever do—as they did in the 1992 anti-liquor movement in Andhra. The patriarchy that operates among the Dalitbahujans operates between two political beings and hence it still retains an element of democracy in contrast to the authoritarian patriarchy of Brahminism. In other words, Dalitbahujan patriarchy is a loose structure which can be demolished with counter-cultural movements more easily than brahminical patriarchy, which is rooted in a spiritually underwritten authoritarianism and which can therefore easily be turned into fascism.

HINDU POLITICAL INSTITUTIONS AND DALITBAHUJANS

Over and above these civil societal political structures, power begins to operate in the state institutions that have come into existence in the villages. In these institutions the Dalitbahujan castes are systematically excluded from the exercise of power. The three important institutions through which village politico-economic power connects itself with other state agencies are the institutions of police, patel or patwari (village police, administrative official and revenue official). Though these institutions are slowly being replaced with gram panchayats, the right to be patels or patwaris is reserved for the Brahmins and the neo-Kshatriyas. As a rule Dalitbahujans are excluded from gaining the expertise to handle these institutions. When these institutions were replaced with gram panchayats the brahminical castes monopolized the panchayats also. With the exclusion of Dalitbahujan castes, the exclusion of Dalitbahujan women becomes automatic. Given Hindu notions of power, 'upper' caste women are also not supposed to take on these functions. Thus these institutions become the preserve of 'upper' caste men. It has been decided recently to set aside 30 percent reservation of posts in gram panchayats and other local bodies for women. Thus, women may get some share in rural power structures, but it does not change their position substantially. Given the low level of rural women's education and poverty, they will gain only ornamental power.

Hinduism runs as a thread in a garland in shaping all institutions as 'upper' caste preserves. Given the authoritarian patriarchal home life of the Hindus, whether it is the patel-patwari institution, or modern institutions like gram panchayats which combine liberal-democracy with authoritarianism, in essence they are embryos of 'upper' caste dictatorship. Elections become a form that can be used to retain real power in the hands of Brahmins and neo-Kshatriyas. By and large the Baniyas operate only within the domain of the market, but the extraction of surplus in the market is closely related to these power structures. In the modern and post-colonial periods, the Brahmins extended their tentacles over political institutions that are gradually modernizing while maintaining their hold on an expanding spiritual domain. Even in the national context, Brahmins have the monopoly over power structures in every sphere. The most powerful position in the village, that of the patwari, is even now a preserve of the Brahmins. The institutions that handle law and order are left to the neo-Kshatriyas. This gives the neo-Kshatriyas enormous control over caste-divided village society. They use the power to acquire control over the land. However, the emergence of neo-Kshatriya political power did not in any way undermine the hegemonic control of Brahmins and Baniyas.

As I discussed earlier, in the context of the politico-economic and spiritual assimilation that was taking place among casteist social forces, a kind of all-India 'upper' caste supremacy had begun to emerge. By 1947 itself an all-India 'upper' caste elite—the new *bhadralok* (the 'upper' caste combine)—was ready to take over the whole range of post-colonial political institutions. From the village institutions of patel and patwari to tehesil offices, collectorates, state and central secretariats; from gram panchayats to municipalities, zilla parishads to state legislatures and the central Parliament, each institution was made the preserve of the 'upper' caste forces, with Brahmins being in the lead in many of these institutions. The neo-Kshatriyas, while coexisting with them, accepted their hegemonic role in law-making and interpreting history.

In the context of anti-colonial, nationalist movements, institutions and organizational structures like political parties and the so-called social organizations emerged. Brahminical forces hegemonized these too, and maintained a leading role for

Brahmins themselves. With the establishment of the Communist Party of India (CPI), the same 'upper' caste bhadralok continued to control power. The hegemonization of these modern institutions by the upper castes became possible because the British colonialists themselves saw a possibility of manipulation of institutions, parties and organizations if they remained in the hands of the so-called upper castes. Therefore, they helped these forces to play the double role of articulating the national interest, which in essence became bhadralok interest, and opposing colonialism in a limited form. Of course, with this objective colonial authority also gave preferential treatment to right wing ideology and undermined left wing ideology. If the colonial authority had wanted to create a strong, anti-brahminical social base, it could have done so very easily. The brahminical bhadralok and the colonial rulers both wished to preserve the status quo. Even so-called democratic intellectuals like Raja Rammohan Roy, Rabindranath Tagore, Ranade, Gandhi and Nehru were propped up by the British. Consciously or unconsciously, the British themselves helped to construct a 'brahminical meritocracy' that came to power in post-Independence India.

THE DALITBAHUJAN REVOLTS

At the same time, it is also true that British colonialism itself provided a ground for emerging Dalitbahujan, organic intellectuals in states like Maharashtra, from where anti-Brahmin ideologies began to emerge. Mahatma Jyotirao Phule, the initiator of the modern anti-Brahmin movement, and Dr. B. R. Ambedkar, the initiator of the nationalist anti-caste revolution, were products of these revolutionary forces. This was a spillover effect of the education system that defined knowledge in altogether different terms from those of brahminical-Sanskrit ideologies. The Ambedkarite anti-caste philosophical school punctured Hinduism as well as brahminical hegemony in the post-colonial period. Ambedkar was the first thinker, in three thousand years of Indian history, who emerged from the house of a Mahar and caused a revolution to occur in the minds of the Dalitbahujans. He helped them revolt against the casteized slavery of India. Ambedkar drew on the philosophy of Gautama Buddha, as against the pretensions of Gandhi, who picked up the brahminical notion of 'Ramarajya' to change the power relations slowly but surely. Ambedkar's political decision, not to join any party that was headed by a Brahmin, a Baniya or a neo-Kshatriya, and his attempt to create his own political and organic intellectual force to bring about an anti-caste revolution, shook the foundations of Hinduism.

How do we judge the Ambedkarite revolution as against the much propagated Indian versions of Communist revolution? It is universally known that Marxism is the most revolutionary theory that capitalist Europe has produced. If only colonial rule in India had produced anti-Brahmin, organic, Dalitbahujan intellectuals who would have been the recipients of the revolutionary theory of Marxism, by now perhaps India would have undergone a Dalitbahujan socialist revolution. Hinduism would have been yesterday's religion and Brahminism would have been the ideology of yesterday. But much to the good fortune of Hinduism and Brahminism, even colonialism helped the structures and philosophical notions of Brahminism by constantly producing and promoting only traditional 'upper' caste intellectuals. In this atmosphere the most revolutionary theory—Marxism—fell into the hands of most reactionary social forces—the Brahmins, the Baniyas and the neo-Kshatriyas. Because of the nexus between brahminical forces within the revolutionary movement, and the brahminical forces operating from outside, that is, bourgeois parties and Hindu institutions, the revolution has not only been delayed, it has been subverted, time and again. The power relations between Communist and non-Communist brahminical forces appeared to be antagonistic but the social relations remained nonantagonistic. The inimical forces had friendly roots and it was the roots that determined the outcome of events.

In the 1980s and 1990s, of course, Dalitbahujan intellectuals who have emerged from the context of Ambedkarite theory and practice are attempting to break new ground to displace brahminical forces and seize power structures in all spheres. This post-colonial development will restructure power relations in altogether unforeseen forms. The process was initiated in the 1990 Mandal struggle. The Mandal and anti-Mandal struggles in a way reflected the beginning of an all-India caste struggle. The Hindutva school and the patriarchal family of the Sangh Parivar realized the danger of an all-India caste struggle breaking out. The Mandal struggle was the precondition for the Dalitization that would weaken and gradually destroy brahminical Hinduism. Therefore, they quickly reorganized themselves to divert the caste struggle into communal warfare. The destruction of the Babri Masjid in December 1992 is a result of such diversionist strategies. The bhadralok forces that were operating outside the Sangh Parivar contributed to strengthening the Hindutva forces in several ways.

In post-colonial India, in the name of Congress democratic rule, the Hindus came to power both at Delhi and at the provincial headquarters. Parliamentary democracy in essence became brahminical democracy. Within no time the colonial bureaucracy was transformed into a brahminical bureaucracy. The same brahminical forces transformed themselves to suit an emerging global capitalism. They recast their Sanskritized life-style to anglicized lifestyles, reshaping themselves, to live a semi-capitalist (and at the same time brahminical) life. Their anglicization did not undermine their casteized authoritarianism. All apex power centres in the country were brahminized and the power of the bureaucracy greatly extended. Because of their anglicization quite a few of them were integrated into the global techno-economic market. Such top brahminical elites were basically unconcerned with the development of the rural economy because it would result in changing the conditions of the Dalitbahujan masses and thus new social forces might emerge. Thus the anglicized brahminical class also became an anti-development social force.

The Hindu brahminical class, working from different centres of power—political parties, bureaucracy and professional structures like courts, hospitals and universities—established a close nexus with the neo-Kshatriyas who were emerging as a kulak class. As I have already said, the neo-Kshatriyas slowly emerged as a class that began to work as a buffer between the anglicized, urban, brahmincal forces and productive castes who became thoroughly marginalized in all power structures. The role of the neo-Kshatriyas is not only historically reactionary but also dangerous in this period of democratic modernity. It will only help the Brahmins and the Baniyas to sustain philosophical, political and economic power while granting a small fraction of it to a section of neo-Kshatriyas. This will again destroy the revolutionary spirit of the Dalitbahujans who have now acquired specific and universal ideologies (Ambedkarism and Marxism, respectively) to overthrow the caste-class hegemony of bourgeois Brahminism. It is only a conscious Dalitbahujan movement which can, step by step, decasteize society, socialize the means of production, and finally create humanitarian socialism in India.

In the past, brahminical forces averted such revolutions by coopting the Kshatriyas who were also part of the Sudra (the term 'Dalitbahujan' was unknown then) revolutions—the Jain and Buddhist revolutions are well known—and hence the change was delayed for centuries. In the modern period too the Dalitbahujan castes of South India who conducted anti-Brahmin struggles almost got co-opted into Brahminism. The tragedy is that at this juncture of history—marked by the 1990 Mandal struggle and 1993 Uttar Pradesh elections—we do not have a single 'upper' caste intellectual who is willing to critique Brahminism. The neo-Kshatriyas think that Brahminism is a necessary instrument for them to retain the power that they have acquired so far and also to climb up the ladder of power. They think that since political power has come to them up to the level of being appointed as Chief Ministers and occasionally even as the President (Sanjeeva Reddy became President of India), it should be possible to capture the Prime Minister's office in future. Even if they achieve that, it does not mean anything because they will have to operate within the ideological and philosophical domains of caste and Brahminism. This means that they liberate no one because the philosophical and ideological power still remains in the hands of the Brahmin-Baniyas. The neo-Kshatriyas have never realized the meaning and role of philosophical and ideological power. For example, why is it that though the neo-Kshatriyas are willing to be co-opted, no neo-Kshatriya has been allowed to become a priest in brahminical temples?

Meanwhile the damage done by the neo-Kshatriyas to the socio-political system is enormous. They are becoming the pillars of Hindutva and of modern fascism. For the anti-caste Dalitbahujan movement the question of the handling of neo-Kshatriyas becomes a delicate task—that of neutralizing them or showing them up as in the camp of brahminical enemies. Having seen their role both in the 1990 anti-Mandal reactionary agitation and also in the 1993 Uttar Pradesh elections, the option left to the Dalitbahujan movement seems to be to acknowledge that the neo-Kshatriyas are with brahminical Hindutva and that they are not being neutralized, much less getting dalitized. In the struggle for establishing Dalitbahujan democracy in India the inevitable conclusion seems to be that the communal Hindu Brahmins, Baniyas and Neo-Kshatriyas seem to be the inimical forces. In fighting these forces, a united front of Scheduled Castes, Scheduled Tribes, Other Backward Classes and minorities seems to be the only hope. And this course has to be followed after resolving many contradictions—which are friendly in nature—in a manner that does not cause friction among these forces.

CHAPTER 4

Contemporary Hinduism

Have post-colonial developments changed the relations between us and the Hindus? Has the notion of social equality, even within the limited domain of the semi-feudal and semi-capitalist economic structures that have gradually been established, changed the socio-economic relations between the Hindus and us?

CASTE AND COLLEGE EDUCATION

As I struggled through the educational institutions, I began to learn that the structures of the state, the country and the world are far larger than those of our village. Later, as I pushed my way into the institutions of higher education at various levels, education began to appear more and more alien to me, more and more brahminical and anglicized. As long as my education remained basically in the Telugu medium, my Telugu textbooks and history textbooks consisted of only brahminical narratives. Even mathematics was taught in a brahminical paradigm. Gods and Goddesses, who appeared in our books were brahminical, the men who were projected as heroes came either from the brahminical tradition or from the Kshatriya tradition. The history books were full of stories of Kshatriya kings: we read their love stories and their war stories; we read about their problems and prospects, their dreams. Dalitbahujan life figured nowhere in the curriculum. We had been excluded from history. In fact, it appeared as if our history was no history at all.

As I entered the B.A. course the medium of instruction shifted from Telugu to English. There were other shifts too. From that point on, even the content of the texts changed. The brahminical framework was replaced by an European one. European systems, whether of religion or society or politics, presented a world which was totally different from the brahminical one. While the brahminical lessons had been conspiratorially silent about our castes and our cultures, the English texts appeared to be doing the opposite. They spoke of classes in Europe, and the textbooks described the cultures of both the rich classes and poor classes. In the English language textbooks we were introduced to writers like Dickens. In political science the cultures of different classes were presented as a part of our study of liberal democratic ideas of 'equality' and 'inequality'.

As I look back, it is clear from the English textbooks that in class societies—which also have conflicting cultures—there is much less of a conspiracy of silence in comparison to caste societies. In the Telugu textbooks the conspiracy of silence is as loud as a thunderclap. A class which is so brazenly casteist in theory and practice is also brazenly silent about its inhumanity in its literary texts. What is amazing is the eulogization of this casteist culture in all the literary texts and the condemnation of our cultures in the same texts. My generation was perhaps the second Dalitbahujan generation to enter higher educational institutions in South India and encounter only 'upper' caste teachers. However radical these teachers were—among them were liberal democrats, left democrats, and even occasionally left radicals—all of them kept silent about the question of caste discrimination, despite the fact that they were practising it day in and day out. They did not perceive brahminical culture as shaping their own existence. They continued to think of Hindu culture as a monolith. Even when they critiqued it, they perceived it only as class culture without realizing that the opposite of Hindu culture is actually Dalitbahujan culture.

Despite their egalitarian ideologies they were not comfortable about people who had names like Ilaiah, Yellaiah, Malliah or Peraiah entering higher educational institutions. Many of them considered most of us as 'undeserving' and felt that our coming into higher educational institutions would only lead to the deterioration of standards. In the opinion of some Hindu teachers we did not deserve a place in the university. Some others argued that we deserved better wages and improved living conditions, but that should happen within the village setting and within the agrarian economy. They felt that instead of pulling down the standards of higher education by pushing us into the educational institutions, we should be provided with improved living conditions within our own setting. In their view we were incapable of becoming proficient in either Telugu or English. Yes, we might not be proficient. That is because neither of these languages reflect our cultural context. Neither of them was structured to engage with issues that are central to our lives. Both languages are alien to us, and the alienness is equally striking in both cases. Moreover, the entire scope of education appears irrelevant. None of the skills we have, nothing of the knowledge we possess, have my place in the system. Worse still, our knowledge is rendered non-existent. Our linguistic skills and our vocabulary become invisible. We have been sitting in hostile anglicized and brahminical classrooms that had been built only by extracting the surplus generated by our own parents.

BRAHMINICAL CIVIL SOCIETY

As we came to urban centres, which were what the expanding towns were, what were the agencies of power and institutions of civil society that we encountered? It was amazing to note that the hotels which were symbols of capitalist melting-pot cultures, where the caste system could have begun to be destroyed, were visibly brahminized. Every other eating-place bore a signboard 'Brahmin Bhojana, Coffee Hotel'. The food prepared in these hotels was cooked according to Brahmin tastes. The non-vegetarian hotels either bore the names of Kshatriya kings or Brahmin-Baniya national leaders. To this day I have not seen in any urban centre a 'Maalaa Hotel' or a 'Maadigaa Hotel' that serves all the non-vegetarian foods—including beef—cooked to suit their own tastes. I have not seen a Kurumaa hotel or a Goudaa hotel that serves the food that suits our tastes. It seemed as though Brahmin and Kshatriya tastes were the universal tastes. All these hotels and shops—even public places like schools and colleges—hung pictures and calendars of the Hindu Gods and Goddesses—Brahma, Vishnu, Maheswara, Lakshmi, Saraswathi, Parvathi, and so on. Not only in the temples where a Brahmin occupies the supreme position of priest and where the *murthies* of brahminical Gods and Goddesses exist, but also in the institutions of civil society such as schools and offices, pictures of the Dalitbahujans are never present. In hotels and shops the pictures or calendars of our Gods and Goddesses are simply not to be seen. As our people moved into urban centres we were forced to feel that there was no place for our culture in public places. Our own people began to feel that if they spoke of Pochamma they would be ridiculed and humiliated. In urban centres the Dalitbahujan masses began to feel that they were actually a minority—at least as far as visibility in markets was concerned.

Of course, even in these urban centres, non-Hindu goods and commodities were being sold by Dalitbahujan shopkeepers, but they were few and quite invisible. One Dalitbahujan caste that was somewhat visible, were the Shalaas (weavers) who were in the cloth trade. They thought that Sanskritization was the only way in which they could survive in the marketplace which had become thoroughly 'baniyaized'. Slowly they began to get Sanskritized. They too began to pretend that they were dwijas by tying a thread around their bodies. They were afraid of putting up the picture of Potuluri Veerabrahmam who was responsible for their social upgradation (in Andhra Pradesh). Even in this urban market, caste occupational relations continued to operate. The Shalaas became mainly retail sellers of clothes. But it must be remembered that the wholesale cloth business slowly shifted almost entirely into the hands of the Baniyas.

The Brahmins, while they extended their socioeconomic and political power to urban temples, educational institutions and public administrative institutions, retained control of the institutions of priest and patwari. The tehesildar, the police sub-inspector, the collector and the superintendent of police were all visible Brahmins who were buying up urban properties, with their salaries (and, more often than not, through their illegal incomes). Slowly the neo-Kshatriyas began to occupy the lower positions in this scheme of power. Here and there, there were also some Scheduled Caste officers, who entered into these positions because of the Ambedkarite reservation policy. Such officers, faced the wrath of brahminical officialdom and of the Baniya business community, while being treated as untouchables in their official circles much as their parents had been in the villages. These officers were becoming a source of inspiration for many of us. They raised hopeful questions in our minds: Why not become like them? While we were students we were not told about the greatness of Phule or Ambedkar who were as competent as Gandhi and Nehru were. We were always told only about Gandhi, Nehru, Subhas Chandra Bose, and so on, people we could never relate to, people whose upbringing had nothing to do with our upbringing. If not this, we were told about Western heroes and thinkers whose lives and ideas too we could rarely relate to. The nationalist movement was presented as a Brahmin-Baniya fight against colonial masters. Nowhere were we told that it was the Dalitbahujan masses who played the key role in driving the British out.

POST-COLONIAL POLITICAL PARTIES

It is important to understand the role of post-colonial political parties. The only two kinds of political parties known to us in our college days were those of the liberal democratic and communist schools. The main political force that represented a liberal democratic political ideology was the Congress. The Congress was systematically moulded into being a bhadralok party. They talked about the welfare of the Dalitbahujan castes, while all the state resources were cornered by the Hindus. The relationship between an 'upper' caste man and a Dalitbahujan caste man within the Congress was like that between Rama and Hanuman. It is common knowledge that Hanuman was a South Indian Dalit who joined the imperial army of Rama to fight against the South Indian nationalist ruler—Ravana. Hanuman worked day in and day out in the interest of 'Ramarajya' (an anti-Dalitbahujan and anti-women kingdom), yet his place in the administration was always marginal and subservient. Similarly, all the Dalitbahujan activists who joined the Congress party were given subservient places in the party hierarchy. Their main task was to mobilize the masses, and organize 'praise *melas*' of 'upper' caste Congress leaders in whose names they would carry the party flag. They would organize photographers to publicize the 'images' of the 'upper' caste leaders. The aim of an average 'upper' caste Congress leader would be to mould every Dalitbahujan into a trustworthy Hanuman. While Ambedkarism was creating a small force of conscious people among Dalitbahujans who were trying to organize themselves into an autonomous political force, a large number were (perhaps for the sake of fringe benefits that the Congress administration could offer, perhaps for other reasons) willing to be Hanumans.

It was thus, that the modern political party system was moulded in the form of a classical social system called Ramarajya. The Congress party, as a liberal democratic party, began structuring itself in a Hindu fashion. The Congress 'upper' caste leaders lived a Hindu life. If there was a Congress Brahmin leader, even at the village and town level, one of his relatives would be the priest in the temple while another relative would be an officer in the government. These people had common political aims and interests at various levels. The nexus between them was total, and they were able to manipulate the system. Their entire life was a modernized Hindu life. But the Dalitbahujans, who by imitating them were trying to get assimilated into this politicized Hinduism or Hindutva, were never allowed to be equal partners. The establishment of a liberal democratic party like the Congress which has ruled this country for nearly fifty years, has not improved unequal caste relations, and the gap between Hindu 'upper' castes and the non-Hindu Dalitbahujans within the party ranks has never been bridged. The relationship always remained antagonistic and distrustful. The distrust is not a result of differing ideologies or loyalties. It is a result of Hindu leaders consistently treating Dalitbahujans as the Other both in religious and cultural terms.

For all the top Congress leaders, the party office provided wealth and social status. A few, very few, Dalitbahujans did acquire wealth, yet they have not succeeded in being assimilated into the Hindu fold. Their status within the upper layers of the party remained very low. The relationship between a rich Maalaa or Maadigaa and a wealthy 'upper' caste person was identical to the relationship between a poor 'upper' caste person and a poor Dalitbahujan. The poor 'upper' caste person thinks that he or she is always superior. Similarly the rich 'upper' caste people also think that they are always superior. Acquiring wealth does not change the relative social status of Dalitbahujans within a particular class. Even within a rich class, caste distinctions continue to operate.

The second major political movement that acquired a social and intellectual base is the Communist movement. The communists have been propagating the theory that the masses are like the sea and that the political movements that arise in society are like its waves and the leaders that emerge in the movement are like the foam. This was the notion propagated by Zhou En-lai, a well-known Communist leader of China. Notionally the Communist leadership was trying to portray itself as an integral part of the masses and to stress that it was no different from the people. But in reality the Dalitbahujan masses and the Communist leadership remained distinctly different in three ways: *(i)* the Communist leadership came from the 'upper' caste—mainly from Brahmins; *(ii)* they remained Hindu in day-to-day life-styles; and *(iii)* by and large the masses were economically poor but the leaders came from relatively wealthy backgrounds. The masses came from Dalitbahujan castes, and these castes never found an equal place in the leadership structures. Even in states like Andhra Pradesh and Kerala, where non-Brahmin movements were strong enough to influence the society, the pattern held good. In Andhra Pradesh the neo-Kshatriyas and some Brahmins like Devulapally Venkateswar Rao and Giri Prasad Rao became leaders, while the mass base (the sea) was from the Dalitbahujan castes. In Kerala the Brahmins, who always remained brutal towards the masses, became the leaders, while the cadre base of the party was from the Dalitbahujan castes. Of course, Bengal is a classic example of rich Bengali bhadralok babus becoming leaders without even mobilizing their own caste people into becoming part of the mass base of the party. All over the country, the Brahmin population has become leaders in all spheres of sociopolitical life. They never remained part of the masses. Thus even the Communist movement started functioning in two separate camps—the 'upper' caste leader camp and the Dalitbahujan cadre camp. Ambedkar was the first one to understand this fact.

Did the Communist 'upper' castes give up the Hindu way of life? Certainly not. Their social relations continued to be within their caste circles. Marriages took place within the caste structure; their 'personal friends' remained within their own caste circles. They never declared themselves to be against Hinduism. They have not built a critique of the Hindu Gods. For example, all the Hindu Gods, beginning with Brahma, Vishnu, Maheswara to the last of the Dashavatara (ten incarnations) were anti-Dalitbahujan weapon-wielding heroes who built a system against Dalitbahujans.

In all of Indian Communist literature, there is no text which has critiqued these Gods. As most of the Communist intellectuals happened to be Brahmins they never really distanced themselves from such Hindu Gods and their culture. Even as the Communists talked about the counter-culture, their counter-culture never distanced itself from Hindu notions of life. This is a unique characteristic of Indian Communists, and it is a result of the caste that the leaders belong to and the Hinduism of which they are a part. They may say that they do not go to temples as ordinary Brahmins or Baniyas do, but they simply forget the fact that they have converted their central committees into Hindu-power management centres. They converted Marx, Engels and Lenin into 'Communist Gods' where people were supposed to find solutions in their theories for every social, economic or political problem that Indian casteist society was suffering from. Persons coming from Dalitbahujan castes were not allowed to become self-confident leaders. It is a brahminical Hindu strategy to destroy the basis of that self-confidence in Dalitbahujan masses.

The philosophical perception of a liberal Hindu leader and a Communist Hindu leader about the Dalitbahujans is similar to that of the classical Hindu forces. They believe that the Dalitbahujans are unworthy of handling power or operating power structures; they believe that the 'upper' castes cannot be led by the Dalitbahujan castes. It never struck a Hindu Communist that the so-called Sudra Gods and Goddesses are quite contrary to the Gods and Goddesses of Hindus. It never struck them that the Dalitbahujan Gods and Goddesses are expressions of the productive cultures of the vast masses. For example, a Kattamaisamma is a discoverer of a tank system, a Pochamma is the discoverer of herbal medicine for all diseases, a Beerappa is the earliest sheepbreeder, a Potaraju the protector of the fields, a Yanadi a steel technologist. A Communist leader should have had a clear perception of cultural differences between the exploiters and the exploited, but these leaders never did care to study these cultures. They felt threatened to discover the production-based culture of the Dalitbahujan castes.

POST-COLONIAL UNIVERSITIES

As late as the 1990s one could see the striking cultural differences between the Hindu castes and the Dalitbahujan castes. In the universities the Brahmins and the neo-Kshatriyas acquired hegemony. In certain universities only the Brahmins are in control of everything. Whether it is medicine, or engineering or scientific research centres or social science educational research departments, or arts faculties, the socio-cultural behaviour of the Hindu 'upper' caste teachers and students and the Dalitbahujan students and non-teaching staff, who entered these institutions, was distinctly different.

When I started teaching in Osmania University I began to realize that no amount of scientific education and Western exposure actually changed Hindus into rational beings. Modern science has not made any impact on them. One reason for this is they have never lived amidst the productive fields. They have never undergone the life experiences that an average working Indian has undergone. Therefore they do not understand the meaning or value of knowledge that emerges from work. This is one of the reasons w hy they continued to argue even as late as 1990 (at the time of the Mandal movement), that youth who come from the Dalitbahujan castes are less meritorious and therefore do not deserve teaching jobs in universities. To our surprise we realized that an average Hindu teacher is an irrational being who does not understand that knowledge is rooted in productive castes, which gives rise to creativity. In comparison, an average Dalitbahujan teacher is a rational being because he never believed in the principle of merit. In his/her view, it is work that produces merit. It appears that the Hindu notion of life gave rise to irrationality that defined everything in inverse order. That is why it is almost impossible to convince an 'upper' caste mind that Dalitbahujan productive knowledge is much more valuable than brahminical textual knowledge. Brahminical notions of knowledge are book-centred. Because of their Vedic background, 'upper' castes perceive knowledge as reading and reciting. In the process they have rendered all higher educational institutions into textbook recitation centres.

Their parents and grandparents did not regard Dalitbahujans as human beings. They treated tilling the land as a lowly, mean job, weeding as wretched, shoe-making as a dirty occupation of Chandalas. Did these notions change after these people had studied science? No. An average Hindu 'upper' caste person, particularly a Brahmin, thinks that the prayers of their grandparents are both science and art. Hindu teachers rarely developed the courage to conduct a dialogue in the classroom. Dialogue or dialectics have never been in the tradition or life-blood of a Hindu. Hindus do not have the life experiences that lead them to experiment or to take risks, without which scientific knowledge cannot develop. Experimentation and taking risks become possible only when consciousness is grounded in a variety of real-life tasks—tilling the land, lifting bricks, weaving cloth, cutting the hair, making the shoe—all these should be real alternatives for making one's living. A Hindu 'intellectual' working in any centre of education is not mentally prepared for such alternatives.

If the inability to experiment and take risks in order to strike new paths is only an individual problem, a system can suffer such an individual without much loss. But if it is the character of all the hegemonic castes, the system cannot afford the luxury of their leadership and dominance, for the brunt of such a system has to be born by the Others who are constantly engaged in experimentation and risk-taking. In fact the whole risk of experimentation was borne by the Dalitbahujai castes. Thus, science has survived in Dalitbahujan houses in very many ways, but in Hindu houses, in spite of acquiring so many electronic gadgets that help them enjoy modern comforts, the philosophical notion of living itself remains unscientific. For example, an average 'highly educated' Brahmin mind cannot understand the simple scientific principle that inter-caste marriages can substantially improve the health of Indians. A Hindu—particularly a Brahmin—does not understand the fact that their historical experience of interacting with nature is getting minimized as the whole caste group is completely divorced from agrarian productive activity. As modem urbanization increases and the Brahmin population is becoming concentrated in urban centres, their social relations get confined to alienated urban colonies. The Brahmin population does not understand the simple fact that the only way to extricate itself from this alienation is to enter into close social relations with other castes which are part of the process of agrarian production. But this is unthinkable for most of them. The mind of an average Brahmin or Baniya is thoroughly blocked by its Hindu idiosyncrasy.

A Dalitbahujan mind is quite the opposite of this. In spite of three thousand years of violent opposition to its getting educated into letters, the initiative, the effort and the ability that the very first generation of educated teachers, scientists, engineers, doctors and civil administrators coming from the Dalitbahujan castes have shown is unbelievable. In exhibiting the basic skills in universities, colleges, offices, laboratories they are not second to any average Brahmin. Moreover, Dalitbahujan people have an enormous in-built strength to keep their minds open. The amount of experience that each one of us has gained in that long journey from the village-single-teacher-local-dialect school education to acquiring a university master's degree has made every one of us a rich preserve of knowledge. In the long journey from one's familiar village caste waada to urban modern educational centres each one of us had to encounter many cultures, face many contradictions, assimilate several new ideas and unlearn many mythical notions that our castes also were victims of. All this was possible only because we were never bound by the Hindu idiosyncrasies of life.

The mind of a Dalitbahujan person is like the body of a person in a circus. It is ready to learn anything in any condition. But for this make-up of the Dalitbahujan mind, it would have been impossible for us—first generation of educated Dalitbahujans—to acquire the skills that we have acquired today, despite such hostile educational environments.

Thus, whichever institution the Dalitbahujans entered, either through reservation (in South India mostly through reservation) or through other ways, such institutions became the centres of conflict between Hindu irrationality and Dalitbahujan rationality, Hindu closedness and Dalitbahujan openness, Hindu silent violence and Dalitbahujan loud self-defence. Out of this very conflict there seems to emerge a new hope of a rational future for this country. Mainly because of this continuous conflict between closed minds and open minds, at least institutions where such mixed groups are working are becoming more vital and competent institutions. In such institutions dead academic cultures are being challenged, and 'upper' caste hegemony is being broken. In many South Indian institutions SCs, OBCs, STs and minorities and 'upper' caste persons work together. This makes these institutions melting pots in terms of cultures and ideas. It must be remembered that in this country because of the caste system several cultures have existed side-by-side, but separately. Brahminism compartmentalized human thinking and human experience was so badly fragmented that no exchange took place between them. Because of capitalist casteism the situation in the urban centres was worse.

BRAHMINICAL COLONIES

As I have said earlier, there are not only Brahmin hotels, Reddy hotels, Baniya shops, Kamma shops, and so on, but there are also caste streets and caste colonies. The Dalitbahujans have been so diffident that nobody dared to open a Maadigaa hotel, a Chakaali hotel or a Gollaa hotel. Dalitbahujans could enter these 'upper' caste streets and colonies only as servants, milk vendors, vegetable vendors, *tapimaistries* (supervisors of construction work), carpenters, and so on. They were the sellers of the skills, and the so-called upper castes, who were themselves unskilled, were the consumers. By and large the Dalitbahujans live in slums. They are debarred from doing anything that would allow them to improve their socioeconomic position or reach the level of the Brahmin-Baniyas. The Brahmin-Baniyas defined even capitalist-urban markets in caste terms. Irrationality and exploitation were made structures to be valued, while creativity was made to be ashamed of its own existence. This actually rendered our capitalist markets moribund casteist markets. No Dalitbahujan person dares to open a business establishment even in metropolitan cities like Bombay, Delhi, Calcutta or Hyderabad. Madras was the exception because of Dravida Munnetra political power. The Brahmins and the Baniyas never realized the fact that the manipulation of capitalist markets to suit the needs of their own culture and ideology is detrimental to the national interest as this casteized capital is becoming more and more incompetent. Not many of us realized that global imperialism finds it easy to handle these small groups of Brahmins and Baniyas who have monopolized the economy, and manipulate them in the interest of imperial markets. The Brahmins and the Baniyas never feel even distantly related to the masses. Therefore, if their selfish interests are served, they couldn't care less about this country and the people.

CASTEIZATION OF CAPITAL

What Hinduism has done is that through manipulative hier-archization, even in the socialist era, it has retained its hegemony over the managerial posts in the urban centres. In every industry the working masses are Dalitbahujans whose notions of life and work are non-Hinduistic, whereas, the entrepreneurs and managers of the factories—the directors, supervisors, engineers—are Brahmin, Baniya or Neo-Kshatriya. As a result, there is a total cultural divide between the managerial class and the working class. If some factory workers starve or if workers get injured or die because of an accident, the managers do not feel for them because there is no social relationship between them. They are separated not only by class but also by caste. Thus the worker's suffering or death is seen as that of the Other. Thus, alienation between workers and managers is twofold. There is no institution or social organization that forces the managers' families and the workers' families to meet; no institution where, at least an explanation, or repentance, is required. In Europe and in other countries, the church and other religious institutions provide this minimal meeting ground, but in India there is no scope for such interaction in the temple. Brahminical culture never allowed the Malaas and the Maadigaas even to enter the temples.

Thus, even in capitalist production, caste operates, and this is what the 'casteization of capital' means. Such casteization of capital results only in inhuman exploitation. Because of the caste alienation of workers from capital, the nature of exploitation in Indian industries is a hundred times more inhuman and cruel than compared to that of the West. No Brahmin or Baniya entrepreneur feels that the workers are part of his or her Hindu religious culture. No Baniya shopowner in the urban centre feels that the Dalitbahujan employees working in the shop are part of their culture. The priests operating in the huge urban temples, unlike the rural priests, wear trousers, travel from their homes to temples on scooters and cars and use multinational products at home. Yet in terms of cultural consciousness they remain Brahmin patriarchs. In spite of such a modernized material life, their philosophy of life does not accept even the idea of a Brahmin woman becoming a priest, much less a Dalitbahujan becoming one. The Hindu temple is the preserve of Hindu males. The 'upper' caste factory manager or engineer, or the 'upper' caste bureaucrat all think that the urbanized priest has a right to modernize and practise casteism simultaneously.

The urban factory, the urban university, the urban bank and the urban administrative office are all under the control of the Brahmins, the Baniyas or the neo-Kshatriyas. They treat the urban Dalitbahujan employees or workers, the watchman or woman the servant woman or man, the professor, doctor, engineer and the bureaucrat, as the most unwanted people in the urban areas because these people are the enemies of brahminical culture. If they work in these modern institutions they are required to exhibit loyalty to the Brahmins and the Baniyas on a minute-to-minute and hour-to-hour basis as the

Dalitbahujan Hanuman exhibited his loyalty to Rama. But the educated Dalitbahujan Hanumans realize how vulnerable they are to exploitation in several forms. They realize that Rama's interests stood exactly opposite to those of Hanuman, and this realization creates distrust and conflict. The Brahmins and the Baniyas know that the emerging Dalitbahujan consciousness is dangerous and hence they have systematically established their control over markets, industrial capital and other institutions that have come to operate in India during the postcolonial period. Indian capitalism has been converted into caste capitalism. We had hoped that the decolonized Indian capital would make caste dysfunctional by giving us equal rights in politics, in economic institutions, cultural institutions, educational institutions and administrative institutions. But that has not happened. The migration from the rural areas to urban centres has not changed our socioeconomic relations as caste discrimination has been built into every structure.

Even though some of us Dalitbahujans are professors, top bureaucrats, doctors and engineers we cannot rent a house in a Brahmin-Baniya locality. 'Upper' caste landlords or landladies put up boards which read 'house rented only to vegetarians'. 'Vegetarian' is a synonym for 'Brahmin', and this expression is used to drive away all Dalitbahujans from their localities. Even if some Dalitbahujans construct or buy houses in Brahmin localities, such houses are culturally isolated and social relations with the other residents do not develop. Even the children are encouraged to avoid interaction. We need only to listen to the experiences of Dalitbahujans who constructed houses in Brahmin localities to perceive the nature and extent of casteism in urban centres.

SANSKRITIZATION HAS NOT WORKED

Many Dalitbahujans have attempted to Sanskritize themselves. They changed their original names into brahminical names. Muthiahs became Murthies. Gopaiahs became Gopalakrishnas. Their children's names extend to post-Sanskritized Brahminism. Their sons are called Vishnus, Ajays or Vijays. Their daughters are called Swapnas, Sandhyas, Lakshmis and Saraswathis. But all this did not change the heart of urban Brahminism. Whatever name a person has, the urban brahminical forces discover the caste background of a person within days and he or she will be treated accordingly.

Many Dalitbahujans educated their children in English-medium schools. These schools bear names like St. Ann's, St. Thomas, St. Mary, and so on. In these schools, the parents hoped that the Dalitbahujan children and the Hindu Brahmin-Baniya children would be educated on an equal basis. But even here they forgot the fact that the majority of the teachers came from brahminical castes and no textbook ever presented Dalitbahujan culture as an integral part of Indian culture. Further, the moment the children returned home, they were pulled back into the culture of their respective castes. Some of us have tried other methods, like assimilating into 'upper' caste cultures. There are several Dalitbahujan officers, politicians, academics and doctors who try to be more Hindu than the Hindus themselves. They brazenly celebrate Hindu festivals. Even in public they speak of their parental culture as low and mean. They refuse any connection with Pochamma and Maisamma. They condemn these Gods as 'Sudra Devathalu'. Short of turning themselves into twice-born castes, these people make every attempt to Sanskritize themselves.

But this did not dilute caste discrimination in urban centres. Not many, who tried the Sanskritization trick, succeeded in getting an 'upper' caste daughter-in-law or a Brahmin son-in-law. More important than all these, no single Sanskritized Dalitbahujan group can claim that their children have the connections to procure a good job without claiming the reservation for which Phule, Ambedkar and Periyar fought all their lives. The Sanskritization process did not dilute caste identities and caste-based humiliations. Many Dalitbahujans who got Sanskritized later realized the fact that Sanskritization is no solution to Hindu barbarity. This is the reason why Ambedkar embraced Buddhism to build a counter-culture to Hinduism, and Periyar Ramasamy Naiker attempted to establish the hegemony of Dravida culture by attacking Hindu culture and Hindu Gods.

CHAPTER 5

Hindu Gods and Us:
Our Goddesses and Hindus

What is the relationship between the Hindu Gods and ourselves? Did the Hindu brahminical Gods treat us as part of their people, or even as legitimate devotees? Why did Hinduism create the images of many Gods as against the universal ethic of monotheism? Did brahminical polytheism work in the interest of Dalitbahujan masses or did it work in the interest of brahminical forces who are a small minority? Further, what is the relationship between the Dailtbahujan Goddesses and Gods and the Hindus? Did the Hindus respect these deities or worship them? What are the socioeconomic and cultural forms of the Dalitbahujan Goddesses and Gods? Since the majority of the people relate to the Dalitbahujan Goddesses and Gods, isn't there a need to present their narratives? I shall discuss all these aspects in this chapter.

Hinduism has a socioeconomic and cultural design that manipulates the consciousness of the Dalitbahujans systematically. It has created several institutions to sustain the hegemony of the brahminical forces. Through the ages it has done this by two methods: *(i)* creating a consent system which it maintains through various images of Gods and Goddesses, some of whom have been co-opted from the social base that it wanted to exploit; and *(ii)* when such a consent failed or lost its grip on the masses, it took recourse to violence. In fact, violence has been Hinduism's principal mechanism of control. That is the reason why many of the Hindu Gods were weapon-wielders in distinct contrast to the Gods of all other religions. No religion in the world has created such a variety of Gods who use both consent and violence to force the masses into submission. Thus, the relationship between the Hindu Gods and the Dalitbahujans has been that of the oppressor and oppressed, the manipulator and the manipulated. Of course, one of the 'merits' of Hinduism has been that it addressed both the mind and the body of the oppressed.

Brahminical theoreticians have constructed their own theory of consciousness with a specific notion that the majority (bahujan) consciousness is confined to one specific activity and that that consciousness has to be constantly monitored in order to arrest its further growth. If a consciousness is manipulated to become and remain the slave of another consciousness, some day or the other it will rebel. These revolts are mostly suppressed. All religions have worked out strategies to manipulate and contain such revolts by teaching the slaves a so-called divine morality. But no religion has succeeded in suppressing the slaves for ever.

Other religions admitted slaves into their fold, although they suppressed them in the political and economic domains. But the Dalitbahujans never became part of Hinduism.

Hinduism differs from other religions even in terms of the way it has structured its Gods and Goddesses. All the Gods and Goddesses are institutionalized, modified and contextualized in a most brazen anti-Dalitbahujan mode. Hinduism has been claiming that the Dalitbahujans are Hindus, but at the same time their very Gods are openly against them. As a result, this religion, from its very inception, has a fascist nature, which can be experienced and understood only by the Dalitbahujans, not by Brahmins who regard the manipulation and exploitation as systemic and not as part of their own individual consciousness. But the reality is that every 'upper' caste person takes part in that exploitation and manipulation and contributes towards the creation and perpetuation of such cultures in the Indian context. The creation and perpetuation of Hindu Gods is a major achievement of this culture.

In the face of the Dalitbahujan revolts, the brahminical forces of India invoked their Gods to suppress the consciousness of the revolt. The most obvious and immediate example in the all-India context, is that of the Hindu response to the implementation of the Mandal report in 1990. The 'upper' castes opposed the reservations to OBCs with all the strength at their command, and the Hindutva movement was organized mainly to oppose the pro-reservation movement. Hence, unless one examines in detail how all the main Hindu Gods are only killers and oppressors of the Dalitbahujans, and how the Dalitbahujan castes have built a cultural tradition of their own, and Gods and Goddesses of their own (who have never been respected by the brahminical castes), one cannot open up the minds of the Dalitbahujans to reality.

THE BRAHMINICAL GODS AND GODDESSES

The head of the brahminical Gods, Indra, is known as the *Deevatideeva*. He is the original Aryan leader who led the mass extermination of the Indus valley based Adi-Dravidians, who were also Adi-Dalitbahujans. Brahmins consider him a hero because he killed hundreds and thousands of Dalitbahujans at that time. After conquering the Dalitbahujans, he established a pastoral Aryan kingdom. In this kingdom, he did not organize people into production, he merely established a big harem. Enjoying the pleasures of that harem and dancing and drinking were his main tasks. Ramba, Urvashi, Tilothama who are again and again symbolized as representing Hindu beauty and Hindu ideals of service were part of his harem. He might have also been a seducer of many Dalitbahujan women which is probably why brahminical literature constructs him as a powerful *Kaamaabhimaani* (one who enjoys sex) hero. But the most important aspect is that he was the main political leader of the Aryans. It was he who led them to political victory. This leader was first and foremost a killer and an exploiter of Dalitbahujans.

BRAHMA AND SARASWATHI

The most important Hindu God—the first of the three murthies— is Brahma. Physically Brahma is represented as a light brown skinned Aryan. He bears the name of Brahma, which means wisdom. Sometimes he is shown as a person who has four hands, sometimes as one who has only two hands. This God of wisdom is armed with weapons to attack his enemies—the Dalitbahujans. He was the one who worked out the entire strategy of war designed to defeat the Adi-Dalitbahujans. It was he who was responsible for the reconstruction of brahminical society. The Brahmins have worked out the social divisions of caste by claiming that they were born from his head, Kshatriyas from his chest, Vaisyas from his thighs and Sudras from his feet. Such an explanation gave a divine justification for the four classes—which have come to be known as the four *varnas*. Subsequently these classes—particularly the Sudra-slave class—were divided into further castes so that class revolt could be curbed once and for all. Brahminical theoreticians—Kautilya, Manu, Vedavyasa and Valmiki—all worked out mechanisms that structured these castes/classes basically in the interest of the brahminical forces. As we have seen in earlier chapters, it is because of this ideological hegemony that the brahminical order—in philosophy, economy and politics—could be maintained from ancient times to the present age of post-colonial capitalism.

Brahma's wife is known as Saraswathi, which also means learning. The construction of the Brahma-Saraswathi relationship takes place strictly within the philosophical bounds of patriarchy. Brahma himself is shown as the source of wisdom in the Vedas, the early Brahmin writings, which were designed to subordinate the native masses of India. The Vedas themselves express the mixed feelings of crude Brahminism. But since they were written by the Brahmins (i.e. by the early literate Aryans), the texts go against Dalitbahujans. In fact, they are anti-Dalitbahujan texts. The absurdity of Brahmin patriarchy is clear in these texts. The source of education, Saraswathi, did not write any book as the Brahmins never allowed women to write their texts. Nowhere does she speak even about the need to give education to women. How is it that the source of education is herself an illiterate woman? This is diabolism of the highest order. Brahminism never allowed women to be educated. The first woman who worked to provide education for all women is Savithribai Phule, wife of Mahatma Phule, in the mid-nineteenth century. To our Dalitbahujan mind, there is no way in which

Saraswathi can be compared to Savithribai Phule. In Savithribai Phule one finds real feminist assertion. She took up independent positions and even rejected several suggestions made by Jyotirao Phule. Saraswathi, the Goddess, never did that. Her husband, Brahma, is a Brahmin in all respects—in colour, in costumes—and also in the alienation from all productive work. He was responsible for manipulating the producers—the Dalitbahujans—into becoming slaves of his caste/class. Whenever the need arose he never hesitated to initiate a bloody war against the Dalitbahujan masses.

Leave alone the ancient and medieval periods, even in the twentieth century, Hindutva attempts to seduce us into accepting this first enemy of Dalitbahujans as our prime deity. The manipulator of knowledge is being projected as knowledge itself. But there are two kinds of knowledge: *(i)* the oppressor's knowledge and *(ii)* the knowledge of the oppressed. Brahma's knowledge is the oppressor's knowledge. The Dalitbahujans have their own knowledge, reflected in several of the ideas of the Charvakas (Dalitbahujan materialists) of the ancient period. The ancient Brahmins hegemonized their knowledge and marginalized the knowledge of the Dalitbahujan Charvakas, using the image of Brahma. Brahma, thus represented the Brahmin patriarchs, and Saraswathi represented the Brahmin women who had been turned into sexual objects.

Saraswathi is also a contradictory figure. Though she was said to be the source of education, she never represented the case of Brahmin women who had themselves been denied education, and of course she never thought of the Dalitbahujan women. She herself remains a tool in the hands of Brahma. She becomes delicate because Brahma wants her to be delicate. She is portrayed as an expert in the strictly defined female activities of serving Brahma or playing the veena—always to amuse Brahma. Brahma is never said to have looked after cattle, or driven a plough; similarly, Saraswathi never tends the crops, plants the seed or weeds the fields. She is said to have become so delicate that she could stand on a lotus flower. She could travel on a *hamsa* (a swan, a delicate bird). This kind of delicateness is a negative delicateness. It only shows that her alienation from nature is total. In order to live this alienated but luxurious life, the Brahmins have built up an oppressive culture. That oppressive culture was sought to be made universally acceptable.

VISHNU AND LAKSHMI

The second God who is said to have played a predominant brahminical role, yuga after yuga, is Vishnu. Why is Vishnu said to have been a blue-skinned God? The reason is quite obvious: He is the projection of an association between the Brahmins and the Kshatriyas. This godhead might have been created at a time when the Kshatriyas (a hybrid caste that might perhaps have emerged in cross-breeding between white-skinned Aryans and dark-skinned Dravidian Dalitbahujans) were in revolt against the Brahmins. Jainism and Buddhism were perhaps the last of such revolts. Vishnu is said to be the upholder and preserver of all the principles that Brahma evolved. He is assigned the task of preserving and expanding Brahmin dharma. He wields the *vishnuchakram*, an extremely dangerous weapon, designed to injure all those who rebel against the Brahmins. He is supposed to be merciless in suppressing revolts. Interestingly, he is shown sleeping on a snake which suggests his wickedness more than it does his humanism. For an average Dalitbahujan the snake symbolizes evil, not virtue. He is monogamous as he is married to Lakshmi. The relationship between Lakshmi and Vishnu is no different from that between Brahma and Saraswathi. Lakshmi is supposed to aid Vishnu in his anti-Dalitbahujan designs. Her role is very clear: she must keep pressing the feet of Vishnu as he lies cogitating about the prosperity of Brahmins and the destruction of the Dalitbahujans. She is supposed to procure wealth and victory for the Brahmins, the Kshatriyas and the Vaisyas. But she must also keep a watch on Dalitbahujans. If she comes to know that a Dalitbahujan man or woman has acquired wealth or is revolting against the caste system, she is required to bring that to the notice of Vishnu who will go and exterminate such persons.

Brahminism is so diabolical that even Brahmin and Kshatriya women are assigned significant roles that keep the Dalitbahujans suppressed. Saraswathi must see to it that the Dalitbahujans do not become literate and ensure that they can never understand the brahminical methods of manipulation. Lakshmi is assigned the role of alienating Dalitbahujans from private property: land, gold and other metals. In other words, the Brahmin woman is supposed to see that the Dalitbahujans are denied the right to education and the Kshatriya woman is assigned the duty of denying the right to property to Dalitbahujans. These kinds of roles for 'upper' caste women have played an important part in assimilating them into Brahminism—but as unequal partners. In fact, as Phule repeatedly said, Brahmins were so cunning that they have assigned to Lakshmi the role of being the source of wealth and property while all Brahmin women are denied the right to property. As in the case of Saraswathi, Lakshmi, the source of wealth, is herself a poor dependent.

Assigning these roles to women has had a double-edged function. Within the caste, gender roles are strictly defined but even the oppressed gender is assimilated into the opposition against the other caste/class. Brahmin and Kshatriya men play the role of producing knowledge that lies outside the domain of production, and through which the enemies of brahminical consciousness are controlled. As a result, Dalitbanujan consciousness itself is made to consent to its oppression. If the consent system is broken, the Kshatriya God—Vishnu—is always vigilant to suppress the offenders by using violence. By creating such images of the Gods and Goddesses—Indra, Brahma, Saraswathi, Vishnu, Lakshmi—the possibility of breaking the brahminical system was arrested from several aspects: knowledge, wealth and war being predominant.

It is not very clear why Vishnu and not Brahma was chosen to be reincarnated in different forms at different times to suppress Dalitbahujan assertion. Perhaps it was because the Kshatriyas already wielded political power, but it was important to make the Kshatriya kings acquiesce in their subordination to the Brahmins. If such a message emerges from the Kshatriya Gods and Goddesses themselves, building up consent from the Kshatriyas becomes easier. To a large extent that purpose was also served because through the message of Vishnu and Lakshmi the Brahmins ensured their philosophical and ideological hegemony even over the

Kshatriyas, and through the message of Lakshmi even while being out of responsible positions of running the state or conducting wars, the Brahmins could acquire wealth for the mere asking. More important, the Dalitbahujans were suppressed year after year, century after century and yuga after yuga.

The influence of the figures of brahminized women like Saraswathi and Lakshmi is enormous on 'upper' caste women in India. The image of Lakshmi gets reinforced day in and day out since she is said to be the source of wealth. During the 1990 Mandal debate many well-known women writers began to feel insecure and opposed the anti-caste movements without even realizing that these were in essence anti-caste movements. Internalization of personalities like Lakshmi and Sita by 'upper' caste women have several implications for Dalitbahujan movements and also for women's movements. In a casteized patriarchal system Dalitbahujan movements and women's movements should extend helping hands to each other. Such coordination becomes possible only when 'upper' caste women overcome the influence of Brahminism, which restrict their worldview. It is unfortunate that no women writer, not even feminists, have deconstructed the socio-political influences of these Goddesses on women—particularly on brahminical women.

SHIVA AND PARVATHI

The third among the *trimurthies,* the one who is least powerful, and who is easily fooled, is Shiva or Maheswara. In terms of colour and costume he neither resembles Brahma and the Brahmins nor does he resemble Vishnu and the Kshatriyas. He is dark-skinned and dressed like a tribal. Though this God is associated with Brahma and Vishnu, he is assigned a third position and he does not have as defined a role as Brahma and Vishnu do. Though he is also powerful and wields the *trishula* as his weapon, basically he plays the subordinate role to Brahma and Vishnu. His behaviour is a little different from that of the Brahmin and the Kshatriya Gods. He loves dancing and gets himself into all sorts of difficulties from which he needs to be rescued by Brahma or Vishnu. The story of Bhasmasura is a good example of Shiva's dependence on Vishnu.

His wife, Parvathi, or Gauri as she is also called, also does not have as specific a role as Saraswathi or Lakshmi. She joins her husband in many of his activities. They dance and roam around. But Parvathi, unlike Saraswathi and Lakshmi, questions many of the activities of her husband. She also plays certain roles which do not, strictly speaking, fall within the domain of ritual Hinduism. Perhaps this couple comes from a tribal origin. On the whole, however, Parvathi supports Saraswathi and Lakshmi in their anti-Dalitbahujan activities. The question is, then, for what purpose was the image of Shankara and Parvathi constructed? To my mind there is a definite purpose in these images. The images of Brahma, Vishnu, Saraswathi and Lakshmi were enough to control the minds of those Dalitbahujans, Vaisyas and Kshatriyas who have already come into the grip of brahminical civil society. These four figures were adequate for ensuring Dalitbahujan consent or, when necessary, suppression. This was because, by and large, the theory of karma had already been universalized among them, although, as I said in earlier chapters, these Gods were not at all known to the Dalitbahujans. To the extent that they were known, the concept of karma has created an ideological preserve of consent, and worked to ensure that the Dalitbahujans did nothing to challenge their hegemony.

What had become problematic and unmanageable, as far as the tribal population was concerned was that slowly but surely they were being pulled into brahminical civil society. However, they did not identify with Brahma and Vishnu, who looked different from them. These Gods were not adequate for creating a consent base among the tribals. So the Brahmins constructed these two images as God and Goddess who were tribals but had accepted the hegemony of Brahminism in all spheres. Certainly the creation of the images of Shiva and Parvathi was instrumental in creating a consent base among the tribals because Shiva propagates Brahminism and forces people to accept the authority of the Brahmins by violence. These two images were successfully used to subdue the tribals. This is a part of the brahminical theory and practice of 'co-optation.'

The assimilation of Shiva, however, also created its own problems for Brahminism. Over a period of time, the tribals—particularly of South India—were being coerced into the Hindu brahminical system. But the people who came from this tribal background also created friction in Hinduism by asserting autonomy for themselves as the cult of Shiva was relatively more liberal than that of Vishnu. While Vaisnavism became an increasingly fundamentalist Brahminism, Shaivism became a liberal school of Hinduism. With the emergence of Basava's Veerashaiva movement, Shaivism posed a challenge even to Hindu Brahminism. But during the nationalist period the Hindutva school systematically resolved these contradictions among themselves by projecting the notion of a monolithic Hindutva. And as of today, the Shaivite Hindutva is as anti-Dalitbahujan as the Vaisnavite Hindu Brahminism. Of course, the militant Hindutva that was resurrected during the 80s and the 90s closed these ranks totally and presents itself as a monolithic political force (though the rift between Shiv Sena Hindutva and BJP Hindutva are expressions of the Shaivite and Vaisnavite cults, there is a unity in their use of the Rama image for votes). In future, however, in the face of a modern challenge to Hindutva from educated Dalitbahujans, the unification of Vaisnavite Hindutva and Shaivite Hindutva forces is certain. They will be united both in rebuilding the consent of the Dalitbahujans, and in using force against them. By the time Brahminism created the polytheist trimurthies, it also perfected the art of co-opting images in God forms and excluding the masses from the structure of these images. In this way the ultimate objective of subordination and exploitation of the vast masses was achieved to a large extent.

THE AVATARA GODS

Though the trimurthies and their wives had achieved the main objective of the Brahmins, Dalitbahujan revolts continued to take place. As a result, Brahmins went on creating more and more God and Goddess images through the technique of *avataras*. From among the later avatara Gods and Goddesses, Vamana, Krishna,

Rama and Sita are important. Though Phule and Ambedkar did build up a 'Sudra' critique of some of these avataras, it is important to extend this analysis in the light of post-colonial Hindutva. Of the ten so-called avataras of Vishnu, the Buddha is an obvious co-optation. Even an average, urban-educated Indian knows this and therefore, I do not need to analyse the question of the Buddha.*

VAMANA

Of the remaining avataras, three are important for our purpose—Vamana, Krishna and Rama. Like many historians, I am also of the opinion that the *Ramayana* was written after the *Mahabharatha*. After Brahma, Vamana is the only God who was said to have been born as a Brahmin. In setting up the story of the origin of this God the Brahmins have not been so intelligent. The narrative depicts Vamana as being incarnated to kill the Dalitbahujan king, Bali Chakravarthi, who did not believe in Hindu Brahminism and worked to establish a casteless society. Upset by Bali's moves, the Brahmins of the area projected a dwarf Brahmin boy as the incarnation of Vishnu. A great deal of propaganda was done about the capacities of Vamana around that area to enthuse confidence among Brahmins and intimidate the Dalitbahujans. They also announced that on a particular day Vamana would visit Bali. They terrified the Dalitbahujan masses and also Bali with this very propaganda. One fine morning all the Brahmins of the area went to Bali's place along with Vamana. Though Bali was told by his teacher Shukracharya that this dwarf was only a disguised Brahmin, Bali was tempted to believe that he was God. The Brahmins managed to pour acid in Shukracharya's eyes and Bali was rendered supportless.

Vamana asks Bali for three *varas* (gifts). Bali agrees. Vamana asks for three footspans of land. Without realizing its implications, Bali agrees. Then Vamana uses his brahminical trick. He goes up to the top of the building and points one foot towards the sky and declares that the whole of the sky is covered by that foot. Then

---

* See my book *God as Political Philosopher: Buddha's Challenge to Brahminism* (Samya, 2000).

he points another foot towards the earth and says it covered the whole earth. The protests of Bali that such claims are lies are shouted down by the Brahmins around. Vamana then descends from the building and asks for a place for the third foot. Before Bali recovers from the shock of godly lies, Vamana claims that since there was no land to put his third foot he will put it on Bali's head. He breaks Bali's head by stamping on him with his iron-studded footwear. Thus, the Dalitbahujan kingdom was conquered by Hindu treachery and the most humanitarian Baliraja was murdered. Phule in all his writings speaks of the injustice done to Bali by the Brahmins and asks the Dalitbahujans to establish an egalitarian society such as the one in which Bali was the leader. Phule also exposes the Brahmins' inhuman treachery.

KRISHNA

Who is Krishna? Why did the Brahmins create such a God? Why is it that he was said to have been brought up by a Yadava family, though he was born a Kshatriya? Suddenly, and only with regard to Krishna (all other Gods and Goddesses are Brahmins and Kshatriyas), why is such a compromise made? Even Karna who was said to have been brought up in a Dalitbahujan family, though he was born a Kshatriya, is condemned, but not Krishna whose life-story has a similar caste narrative. The accounts of his childhood mischief in cowherd houses, the stories of his promiscuous relationships, and his other nefarious activities—with Radha and other Yadava women—are all projected as divine. Krishna is represented as the guru, leader and war strategist for minority (Pandava) dharma against the majority (Kaurava) dharma. Finally it is the same Krishna who is said to have authored the most brahminical text—the Bhagavad Gita—which became the sacred text of the Hindus, just as the Bible is the sacred text of the Christians, and the Koran of the Muslims. At a time when the Sudras had no right to education, how did a Yadava write the Gita? How did a Yadava writer not provide any social space for Yadavas themselves, leave alone the other Dalitbahujans? There is a need for deliberation on all these questions.

It must be remembered that the epicentre of Brahmin, Kshatriya and Dalitbahujan wars was the present Uttar Pradesh and Bihar region. The Yadavas are the single largest caste in the area. Many revolts against Brahmin-Kshatriyas in these regions were led by them. On several occasions the Yadava community was brutally suppressed along with other Dalitbahujans. But the revolt they led around the period of the *Mahabharatha* seems to have been so tremendous, that Brahmin-Kshatriya forces felt that the consent system that they had built among the lower castes was radically threatened. Once the consent system that sustains the hegemony of a caste/class breaks, it cannot be regained through any number of wars. Take for example, revolts of Dalitbahujans in this heartland of Brahminism around the Mandal struggle as well as the anti-Ramarajya struggle in 1990-1993. The Yadavas of the area took the lead in this struggle. Gradually the alliance between the Scheduled Castes and Backward Classes was worked out, mainly by the Yadavas. In this struggle, the role of B. P. Mandal, a Yadava (who wrote the Mandal Report), Mulayam Singh Yadav and Laloo Prasad Yadav who are for Mandal Raj and are against Ramarajya are well known. This happened because the Yadavas took the lead in breaking the consent structure of the Hindu-brahminical hegemony. As against this the brahminical BJP co-opted two leaders from the Lodha caste—Kalyan Singh and Uma Bharathi. This is done only to ensure that the Brahmin hegemony can be sustained by capturing political power through elections. Though Kalyan Singh might have been made the Chief Minister the real power remained with the Brahmin pandits. This is an example of modern co-optation.

The Hindu-brahminical forces, however, broke the alliance between the SCs and the OBCs by working out much more dangerous strategies of co-optation. The Bharatiya Janata party, as a part of this strategy, extended its support to Mayawati, a woman leader of the Bahujan Samaj party. She is an excellent organizer and a powerful orator. The BJP wanted to help her to remove Mulayam Singh Yadav from the Chief Ministership. Thus, in July 1995 the BJP supported her to become the Chief Minister. Once again, the Yadavas were projected as a most dangerous people. The BJP made a serious attempt to break the alliance between the OBCs led by the Yadavas and the SCs by appearing to be willing to co-opt the SCs who had suffered most at the hands of Brahminism. Of course, they wanted to make this co-optation without altering the SCs socioeconomic and political position.

Mayawati and Kanshi Ram, the president of the BSP, saw through the game. They fought the brahminical designs over the Mathura temple and Masjid issue after Mayawati was installed as Chief Minister. The BSP leaders also saw through the brahminical opposition to installing Periyar E. V. Ramasamy statue in Lucknow. It was Periyar, after all, who had exposed the anti-Dalitbahujan nature of the Hindu Gods more than anybody else. The BSP organized several Periyar melas. As Chamars, Mayawati and Kanshi Ram have already withstood attempts at co-optation. This does not mean that Brahminism will give up its co-optation strategies. As it has already succeeded in breaking the alliance between the SCs and the OBCs, it will keep trying to defeat the Dalitbahujans. Through all these attempts contemporary Brahminism is searching for Dalitbahujans who are willing to be projected to play its role and enable the caste system to survive.

Similarly, even in the period of the *Mahabharatha,* the Brahmins needed to project a person who could rebuild a consent system to contain the Yadava revolts. The Brahmins created an image of one who was said to have been born and brought up among the Yadavas themselves, but they had to ensure that it would not result in having to include the entire Yadava community as had happened in the case of the Kshatriyas. If this happened, it would result in expanding the number and scope of brahminical castes. That itself would endanger the hegemony of the Brahmin-Kshatriyas. In order to overcome this problem they worked out the strategy of creating a Krishna (dark blue in colour) who was said to have been born in a Kshatriya family and brought up in a Yadava family. But the narrative is cleverly manipulated. The young Krishna grows up in Yadava culture, but the political Krishna never identifies himself with Yadava culture. His political role is that of a Kshatriya, defending brahminical dharma.

In no single incident did he stand by the Dalitbahujans. It did not matter whether his beloved was a Yadava-Radha or whether the other gopikas were Yadavas. All his legal wives were Kshatriya women. That fitted very well into the brahminical patriarchal culture of having sexual relations with Dalitbahujan women but marrying only women of their own caste. Krishna is the only avatara who is presented as a believer in polygamy. He had eight wives and all of them were Kshatriya women. He is represented as having assimilated some aspects of Dalitbahujan (Yadava) culture—and that part of his character is attributed to his 'Dalitness'. All his brahminical characteristics are attributed to his 'Kshatriyaness'. With Krishna's avatara the Brahmins played their politics extremely well.

The crux lies in Krishna's role in building a strong consent system that drew in all the Dalitbahujans to cement Brahminism. The *Mahabharatha* narrative itself was built on a very strong Kautilyan imagination. That seems to have been a period when the majority, that is, the Bahujans, revolted against the minority to acquire control of land. The fight was between the minority Pandavas (Brahmins, Kshatriyas and Vaisyas were always a minority—they constitute only 15 percent of the population) and the majority Kauravas. There were five Pandavas and a hundred Kauravas. The hundred Kauravas stood against brahminical dharma and represented Dalitbahujans, the majority; whereas the five Pandavas stood for brahminical dharma and represented the brahminical minority. In the fight for land (and for the kingdom) Krishna stands by the minority. Not only that, he plans the whole strategy of the minority war against the majority and uses all the unscrupulous brahminical tricks to defeat the majority.

In this war Karna and Krishna represent two different values. Karna, though born to a Kshatriya woman, Kunti, owns up to Dalitbahujan culture and tradition as he was brought up in a Dalitbahujan family, whereas Krishna, who was brought up by Yadavas, consciously owns up to the Kshatriya cultural tradition. Even in the war Karna represents the majority whereas, Krishna represents the minority. Krishna was also a weapon-wielding God: he wields a *chakram,* he is also the *yuddha radhasarathi* (chariot driver) of the minority. All the skills of Kautilyan statecraft were exhibited by Krishna in the battlefield. For him the end justifies the means and war resolves all contradictions. In defence of minority dharma he justifies violence, brutality and treachery. Karna was killed only through treachery.

In the story of his *raayabhaaram* (ambassadorship) it was very clear that he failed to win the majority through the brahminical mechanism of consent creation. The majority were not willing to give up the land they had acquired through sweat and blood. Finally Krishna resorts to violence. Some of the members of his camp (like Arjuna) were not willing to indulge in such bloody violence but Krishna forces them to kill anyone—guilty or otherwise— from the majority camp, as they had rebelled against brahminical dharma. It was in defence of brahminical ideology that he taught, as is evident in the Gita, the theory of violence, varnadharma and karma. This is the reason why Krishna was so acceptable to brahminical forces. After the defeat of the majority in the struggle for land the Gita was used to create a much stronger consent system to ensure that no serious revolts emerged from the Dalitbahujan social base. Whenever such attempts were made, either by Yadavas or by other Dalit forces, Krishna's Gita was effectively used to manipulate them into submission. During the freedom struggle the Hindu brahminical forces, particularly Gandhi, propagated the Gita message to build a modern consent system for the continued maintenance of brahminical hegemony in the era of capitalism and democracy.

Fortunately, however, Ambedkar understood the political chicanery of modern Brahminism and developed a critique of Hinduism. His critique of Krishna, in his *Riddles of Rama and Krishna and of the Gita,* must be understood against this background. But for Ambedkar's critique, it would have been difficult to understand the role played by Krishna and by the Gita in brahminical ideology. However, for post-colonial Dalitbahujan ideology, both Gandhian Brahminism and Namboodiripad's Communism are problems. If Gandhi modernized a dying Hinduism, the brahminical Communists undermined emerging Dalitism. In other words, Gandhi Hinduized anti-colonial nationalism and the brahminical Communists failed to see the Hinduization of nationalism. There is, therefore, a need for systematic reassessment of the link between Krishna, the Gita, Gandhi and Namboodiripad, who have 'unity in their diversity'. The diversity is in the form of their consciousness but there is unity in the content of that consciousness. Let us turn, however, to Rama and Sita, the images which played havoc by garnering enormous consent from the Dalitbahujans and the women of India.

RAMA AND SITA

The Brahmins did not mince words when they created the last and the most powerful epic images of the powerful monogamous male and female. Both Rama and Sita were said to have been born in Kshatriya families. Rama is a blue-skinned Kshatriya avatara of Vishnu, and Sita is a pale-complexioned avatara of Lakshmi. Why did the Brahmins create these images by writing the *Ramayana* and what did they expect to achieve through this epic narrative?

In North India, after the Dalitbahujan revolts were suppressed, both through consent and through war, the Dalitbahujans of that area were completely subdued. Varnadharma theory and practice became part of mass consciousness. Even the Jain and Buddhist schools that were antagonistic to Brahmin ideology were completely suppressed. Through the establishment of the Kautilyan state (economic and political) Manu's laws were implemented systematically. Brahmins ruled the roost in the system and even Kshatriya assertion no longer continued with the creation of the image of Krishna and after the writing of the Gita. The consent system was so total that no one could raise a finger against the Brahmins. All sections of the population in North India had been subjugated to such an extent that they had lost confidence in themselves and had given up all hope of change.

The Brahmins thought that this was the right time to expand their hegemony to South India, where the Dalitbahujans were ruling. The kingdoms of Tataki, Shambuka, Vali and Ravana were all Dalitbahujan kingdoms. Some Brahmins claim that Ravana was also a Brahmin. This is nonsense. Ravana was a powerful Dravida Dalitbahujan ruler. He was also a militant Shaivaite. Ravana tried to separate Shaivism from Brahminism and to create an autonomous space for Dalitbahujan Shaivism, which is what Basava finally managed to some extent. He established a powerful kingdom with its capital in Sri Lanka so that he could withstand brahminical aggression. The North Indian Brahmins decided that at a time when their dominance was total in the North, the South Indian Dalitbahujan kingdoms must be defeated and the hold of Brahminism extended. Therefore, they planned an aggression on the Dalitbahujan South. The rishis played a very crucial role in deciding on what steps Rama should take. Vishwamitra and Vashishta were the driving forces in the *Ramayana* narrative. They are known as Rama's *kula gurus,* people whose words must be respected under any circumstance.

Apart from extending the hold of Brahminism to the South, the *Ramayana* narrative is also a means of subordinating women by establishing role models for them. It asserts that a wife must be subordinate to her husband, irrespective of the caste/class nature of the man; that no woman ought to be a ruler since such exercise of political power by women within the subcontinent (even among Dalitbahujans) might influence the brahminical Aryans, who had by then established a strong patriarchal system. Northern Brahminism decided to place gender roles hierarchically into brahminical patriarchy even in South India. The later Brahmins were not at all pleased about the 'unbrahminical' relationships that were made respectable by Draupadi and Radha. Draupadi became a public figure though she had five husbands and Radha was said to have had relations with Krishna, though she was not married to him. It is surprising that Hindus give the name Radha to their female children but not of Draupadi. That is because Draupadi had five husbands. Hindus have no disrespect for a man like Krishna who had eight wives but have no respect for Draupadi who had five husbands. Hinduism respects polygamy but not polyandry. In the period of the *Ramayana,* Hinduism was settling down in patriarchal monogamy. So they decided to institutionalize patriarchal monogamy even among the Dravida Dalitbahujans, because the Dravida region still retained elements of a strong matriarchal tradition. The autonomy of men and women was systemic among South Indian masses. This is clear from the Goddess-centered rituals that are universally in vogue in South India even today.

The *Ramayana* is an ancient account of the aggression aimed at brahminizing the Dalitbahujan society of South India, turning it into a brahminizing patriarchy. With this objective the Brahmin rishies came along with Rama, Sita and Lakshmana, attacked the tribal oligarchies and destabilized several independent Dalitbahujan states. Tataki, the famous Dalitbahujan woman, was killed and her state was brought under Brahminism. Then the famous Shambuka was killed, and his kingdom usurped. The major opposition to Rama's aggression came from the ruler of Kishkinda, a tribal king called Bali. The Brahmins befriended Bali's brother Sugreeva and his nephew Anjaneya and, aided by their treachery, killed the powerful Bali. When a beautiful Dalitbahujan woman, Shurpanaka, wanted to marry Rama, the latter said she should ask Lakshmana. But Lakshmana in response cut off her nose and her earlobes. This incident enraged her brother Ravana. He kidnapped Sita to teach Rama a lesson. Of course Rama uses this incident to mobilize the same tribal Dalitbahujans to attack Sri Lanka. Somehow he reaches Sri Lanka and kills Ravana. With the killing of Ravana the Dalitbahujans of South India were conquered by the brahminical Aryans. In fact, what was worse, was after the defeat of Ravana many Brahmin rishies migrated from the North to the whole of South India, which had basically been a casteless society. It was turned into a caste-based society and the Brahmins established their ideological hegemony over the whole of South India.

Thus, in South India, Brahminism was imposed from above. There was considerable resistance to it in civil society which did not accept or practise the brahminical caste system for a long time. Though South Indian Brahmins have tried to institutionalize the caste system, using both coercion and consent, revolts against the system remained part of the history of South India. Anti-Brahmin movements like the Basava movement (in the thirteenth century) the Vemana movement and the Veerabrahma movement (both in the seventeenth century), the Jyotirao Phule movement, the Narayanaguru movement, the DMK movement, Ambedkar's movement and Periyar's movement finally resulted in the establishment of the Dravida Munnetra state in Tamil Nadu (within the Indian Union). All this is a part of South Indian non-Brahmin consciousness that gradually extended to the North in post-colonial India. The establishment of the Bahujan Samaj party in the North in 1984 is an extension of the anti-Brahmin politico-cultural tradition of the South to the North.

As I have argued earlier, in addition to the anti-Brahmin micro-movements there were also several cultural traditions in civil society which were antithetical to the brahminical tradition, cultural ethos and economic system. As a result, the brahminical tradition remained only a surface system in the South. In fact, if in North India, brahminical Hinduism kept Muslim culture confined to the converts and to the state institutions, not allowing it into civil society, in South India the Dalitbahujan masses did the same to Brahminism. At one level the Brahmin priest kept himself in touch with the Dalitbahujan masses on certain occasions like marriages and deaths and extracted money, food materials, cows and land in the form of dakshina. But at another level, Dalitbahujans retained their cultural ethos, their economic notions of life, and their political and scientific tempers which were distinct.

In order to understand the alternative cultural, economic and political specificities of South Indian Dalitbahujans, we must examine some of the images of the Goddesses and the Gods that the Dalitbahujans have evolved for themselves. Our entire lifestyles and philosophical motivations are closely related to these Goddess/God images even today. The Dalitbahujan cultural ethos of the future needs to be shaped by carefully studying these plural cultural traditions.

DALITBAHUJAN GODDESSES AND GODS

There are several images of Goddesses/Gods, which have caste specificities, or regional specificities but there is a basic characteristic that they hold in common in terms of their contexts and the consciousness they give rise to. The consciousness built around Dalitbahujan Goddess/God images is rooted in production processes. Though the Dalitbahujan imagination has played a role in institutionalizing these images it is also important that these images find their centre in human existence and in the relations between productive forces and nature.

In this sense, the philosophical paradigm in which Goddess/God images are developed among the Dalitbahujan masses is different. Deities do not function as means to subdue a section of society; they are not designed to exploit a section within the community; they function to create a common cultural ethic, one that re-energizes the masses so that they can engage in productive activity. To appreciate the contrast between Dalitbahujan culture and Hindu brahminical culture we should examine the Goddess/God images that are popular among the Dalitbahujan village people. It is important to note that the number of Goddesses are more than that of Gods in the Dalitbahujan narratives.

POCHAMMA

Pochamma is the most popular of Dalitbahujan Goddesses in Andhra Pradesh (I am sure a Dalitbahujan Goddess with similar characteristics exists all over India). Near every village, there is a small Pochamma temple. The notion of temple itself is very different in the case of this Goddess. The temple is a place where the deity exists but not in order that regular pujas be conducted for her. Pochamma is not made the object of a daily puja by the priest. Once every year the masses (and this includes all castes except Brahmins and Baniyas) go to the temple with *bonalu* (pots in which sweet rice is cooked), wash the small stone that represents the deity, and clean the temple and its surroundings. The people can approach the Goddess without the mediation of a priest. They talk to the Goddess as they talk among themselves: 'Mother,' they say, 'we have seeded the fields, now you must ensure that the crop grows well, one of our children is sick it is your bounden duty to cure her . . .

If one listens to these prayers, it becomes clear that these are a very human affair. There is nothing extraordinary about them. The people put small quantities of the *bonam* food (which is known as *padi*) on a leaf in front of the deity. Finally the chicken or sheep they have brought there will be slaughtered. The Dalitbahujans beat the *dappulu* (percussion instrument), while the young people dance and make merry.

What is their notion of Pochamma? She is the person who protects people from all kinds of diseases; she is a person who cures the diseases. Unlike Sita, her gender role is not specified. Nobody knows about Pochamma's husband. Nobody considers her inferior or useless because she does not have a husband. The contrast between Saraswathi and Lakshmi, on the one hand, and Pochamma on the other, is striking. Pochamma is independent. She does not pretend to serve any man. Her relationship to human beings is gender-neutral, caste-neutral and class-neutral. She is supposed to take care of everyone in the village. She herself relates to nature, production and procreation. The closeness of the relationship that exists between Pochamma and the people is evident in the belief that she understands all languages and all dialects. The people can speak with her in their own tongues; a Brahmin can go and talk to her in Sanskrit; an English person can go and talk to her in English.

Before going to Pochamma everyone bathes, and puts on clean clothes. Those who can afford it, wear new clothes. While approaching Pochamma, one does not have to wear a *pattuvastram* (silk cloth), neither does one have to fast the whole day as one would be required to do when approaching the Hindu Gods and Goddesses. People can eat whatever is available in their houses, drink toddy or arrack. This does not mean Pochamma hates vegetarians (like the Hindu Gods hate non-vegetarians now, and hated vegetarians in ancient India). One can go to Pochamma with some vegetarian food and still approach her. As she is a Goddess of the people, she regards the habits of the people with sympathy. As there is no notion of a priesthood among Dalitbahujans, everybody prays to Pochamma in his/her own way. Can a Muslim or a Christian approach her? Yes. There are no restrictions of religion in a Pochamma temple. People can, and do, go to her whatever their religious moorings. Pochamma does not specify what should be offered to her. The offering depends on the economic conditions of the family. The rich take a sari and blouse piece with the bonalu and then take them back to their respective houses. Those who cannot afford such offerings can go to the temple without anything.

Pochamma's temple is not centralized like Rama, Krishna, Venkateswara temples. She is available in every village and people do not have to travel long distances to visit her. All these things have implications for people's social and economic lives, their time and their psychological satisfaction. In other words, the spirituality that emerges around Pochamma does not divide people; it does not create conditions of conflict; it does not make one person a friend and another an enemy. Pochamma is not a Goddess who believes in communal conflicts. Religious distinctions have no meaning for her. If a pig passes by a Pochamma temple, while there are people around, nobody takes objection; no animal, including a pig, is inauspicious in Dalitbahujan culture. There is not a single example of communal riots being initiated from Pochamma temples. Such riots have been initiated from Rama temples, Krishna temples, Narasimha temples, just as riots have been initiated from mosques.

Is Pochamma rooted in materialist culture or is she rooted in *mantric* (magical, auspicious chants) culture? There are a number of mantrics in the villages. They too believe in the power of the other world like the Brahmins do. But the village mantrics do not relate to Pochamma. They are independent persons who claim that they can change the conditions of peoples' lives by calling spirits but certainly no mantric claims that he or she controls Pochamma. Nobody is given a mediating role between Pochamma and the people. The village mantrics jump, dance and untie their long hair and begin to spell out the names of powerful trees and leaves, and names of people who discovered them. All this is known as *Shivamtuluta,* and these mantrics are known as *Shivasathulus.* Sometimes they devote themselves to specific Goddesses. There are Shivasathulus who are devoted to Pochamma. They do not mislead people for the sake of money. They work throughout the day and in the evenings they go into a trance of *shivam* (godliness). They never tell people that they can cure diseases. There are women, too, widows mostly, who believe in the power of the other world! After the day's work is over, they too get into a trance of shivam, and become *Shivasathis.* Then they dance and sing and chant the names of trees and plants and people. In fact, Shivasathi-hood is a social outlet for the widows. Is Pochamma literate or illiterate? Nobody knows the answer to such a question but the fact remains that she is not spoken of in relation to education at all. As the village masses— particularly women—are illiterate, they never relate to her or think of her in connection with education or employment. The demands of the masses basically relate to production, procreation and sickness. In that sense she is more a materialist Goddess, concerned with human life and needs.

KATTAMAISAMMA

A Goddess whose popularity is second only to Pochamma, is Kattamaisamma. Kattamaisamma is a Goddess of water, whose deity (a small stone) is kept on the bund of the village tank. She too does not require a big temple. People believe that Kattamaisamma is responsible for ensuring that the tank is filled. She regulates the water resources. The Dalitbahujans believe that right from the seeding stage to the cutting stage, Kattamaisamma protects the crop. The paddy fields below the tanks flourish because of her blessings. Today, that kind of belief is being slowly eroded. They now think that the quality of the crop depends on fertilizers, and pesticides and hence even an average illiterate peasant uses fertilizers. In that sense, the Dalitbahujan mind is a scientific mind and can easily absorb emerging technology and science. But in spite of this, Kattamaisamma continues to play an important role in their consciousness. A whole range of rituals take place around Kattamaisamma.

Once in five years a major festival focussing on Kattamaisamma is celebrated. In some villages, several sheep, goats and chickens are killed and a big feast is organized. Rice is cooked and soaked in animal blood and sprinkled in the fields as *bali* (sacrifice). The belief here is that Kattamaisamma must see to it that the fields yield good crops and that the crops become socially useful. As we say in our language, it must have *barkati* (prosperous utility).

What is the social origin of Kattamaisamma? A primary investigation will indicate that she was a Dalitbahujan woman who discovered the technology of tank construction. She must have wandered around and studied patterns of land and water very carefully. Perhaps she is the one who found out where to locate a tank, what kind of a bund to construct, and how much water to store. Naturally the discovery of such a system would have boosted agricultural production.

POLIMERAMMA

Yet another important Goddess that the Dalitbahujans have created and popularized among themselves is Polimeramma (the border Goddess). Polimeramma is supposed to guard the village from all the evils that come from outside, to stop them at the boundary of the village. The duty that people assign to her is the protection of the whole village, irrespective of caste or class. Once in five or ten years, a buffalo is killed at the Polimeramma temple and the blood is mixed with a huge quantity of cooked rice, while the meat is eaten by those who eat it—mainly Maalaas, Maadigaas and Muslims. The Muslims are not at all excluded from the ritual. The blooded rice is thrown to all the roof tops as bali. All the agrarian families demand such a bali, but the Brahmins and the Baniyas keep themselves apart. Even the Muslim families demand their own share of the bali, as they are part of the agrarian structure in the village.

Muslim men and women do planting, weeding, cutting of crops along with Dalitbahujan men and women. They share the food that the Dalitbahujans take to the fields. They share their individual agrarian skills. The *Peerila* (Moharram) festival is as much a Dalitbahujan festival as that of Muslims. Dalitbahujans lead the *Peeri* procession. They too hold the *peeri* (a large wooden frame with copper plates on top of it and decorated with colourful cloths called *dattees)* on their shoulders. On festive occasions the *biriyani* (a special food wherein mutton and rice are mixed and cooked) that Muslims cook is sent to Dalitbahujan homes. Thus, the taste of biriyani in Dalitbahujan homes is a contribution of Muslims. In a situation of such close relationship between Dalitbahujans and Muslims all the agrarian festivals of Dalitbahujans are also Muslim festivals. The most popular notion of barkati in Telangana villages is taken from the Urdu word *barkat*. In such a situation of close relationship between the Dalitbahujans and the Muslims, the Muslim demand for bali is an integrated process.

After the bali is sprinkled on the houses, the village is closed for one week from other villages. The idea is that the diseases and evils from other villages must not enter this village. Similarly, for one week, the people belonging to this village cannot go to other villages because such a journey would take away the prosperity of the village. During that period, there are debates about prosperity, about good and evil, all centred around production, procreation and diseases.

OTHER GODDESSES

There are several other village-specific, area-specific, caste-specific Goddesses. Yellamma, Mankalamma, Maremma, Uppalamma, Sammakka, Sarakka are some of them. One important aspect of these Goddesses is that they do not have specific female roles. They are not known for controlling, exploiting or manipulating their husbands nor are they known for subordinating men. None of these Goddesses is said to represent delicate femininity. They are not shown sitting on lotus flowers, not shown travelling on peacocks, or on hamsas or other birds. Not a single Goddess is shown as a woman pressing the feet of her husband like Lakshmi and Saraswathi. Even Dalitbahujan men respect these Goddesses. They are powerful and independent women. The Bengali Kali is depicted as fierce and untamed, dancing over corpses, wearing garlands of skulls. But the Dalitbahujan Goddesses of South India do not represent that kind of violence. They are known as wise women who have discovered something for the well-being of the village; they are people who have saved the village from danger, or who constantly keep watch on the village crops and wealth.

There are Goddesses who got involved in wars to protect the whole area. Good examples are Sammakka and Sarakka, two tribal Goddesses very popular in the Telangana districts. The story of these Goddesses indicates that these militant tribal women opposed the invasion of the Kakatiya kings on the Mulugu tribal belt during the twelfth and thirteenth centuries. Sammakka organized the tribal masses to defend themselves. The mighty Kakatiya army defeated these tribal armies; Sammakka, Sarakka and Sammakka's brother Jampanna were killed near Jampannavagu (near Mulugu, Warangal district). From that point on, Sammakka and Sarakka became the martyr heroines of the tribes. Gradually, the Dalitbahujans from the plains also began to celebrate the *Jatara* (festival).

Though Sammakka and Sarakka emerged as Goddesses from the battlefield, unlike the Hindu Gods, they are martyrs not victors and subduers. It is common for martyrs to be transformed into divine spirits. The story of Christ himself is one example. There is no Hindu God/Goddess who has martyred himself or herself in defence of the masses. All are ultimate winners like the heroes in Hindi and other regional language films. In any narrative in which the hero or heroine is ultimately victorious, violence gets justified and even glorified as a positive cultural ethos. This is the main difference between the Hindu cultural tradition and the Dalitbahujan cultural tradition. In the Dalitbahujan tradition, in no story is violence privileged as it is in Hindu narratives.

POTARAJU

This is true of the God narratives of the Dalitbahujans also. Take, for example, a common village God called Potaraju. Potaraju is very popular among the agrarian castes. Every peasant family keeps a stone painted white and spotted with turmeric in the field.

This deity has no connection with a temple. It hardly occupies one square foot of land while the temples of the Hindu Gods occupy several acres of useful agrarian and housing land. There are very few rituals that are associated with him. The people believe that Potaraju protects the fields from thieves and marauding animals. It is in the security of this belief that no peasant keeps a watch on the crop. This belief works among everyone, so nobody steals a crop since it will invoke the wrath of Potaraju. When a thief sees the image of Potaraju in the field he hesitates to touch anything there. What Potaraju expects from the people in return is very simple. After the crop is harvested, a chicken is sacrificed at the Potaraju image. The people believe that

Potaraju is satisfied by this, and, of course, the chicken curry is relished by the people who do not have to place even a small quantity before the God.

No village Goddess or God expects a *yagna* that involves priests. No *pulihoora, prasaada, daddoojanam, ghee* or *perugannam* are offered to them. No oil, fat or sweets are thrown into the fire to satisfy these Goddesses or Gods. Of late, because of the influence of Brahminism, the peasants do break coconuts (which in fact are a symbol of a clean shaven head with a scalp lock—*pilakajuttu)* to satisfy Gods and Goddesses. Sometimes the broken coconuts and cut limes are thrown on the street corners to get rid of evil spirits. But otherwise no Dalitbahujan celebration involves any wastage of food or other produce.

BEERAPPA

There are a number of caste-specific Gods and Goddesses such as Beerappa (a Yadava God), Katamaraju (a Goudaa God). The stories of such caste-specific Gods tell of the problems that these Gods and Goddesses encountered in building up that particular caste or profession. The narratives also show how these Gods and Goddesses struggled to preserve the cultural tradition of those castes or professions. Take, for example, Beerappa who has a full-length narrative which is told to the people on every festive occasion by expert story-tellers. This story-telling is a ritual that has its own set of musical instruments—*dolu, taalaalu.* The storytellers put on the costume that Beerappa himself was said to have worn. The narrative is accompanied by a dance done in an extremely pleasant rhythm and style. I have not come across a single Brahmin or a Baniya who knows the details of this famous story. But the story of Beerappa was part of our childhood. Many Kurumaa and Gollaa (Yadava) boys treat Beerappa as their ideal, and many Kurumaa and Gollaa girls regard his sister Akkamankali as the ideal woman.

What is the story of Beerappa? Beerappa was an expert sheepbreeder who was not married, though he had reached his twenties. He had lost his mother and father in childhood itself. He was brought up by his sister Akkamankali who remains unmarried to be with her brother. Both Akkamankali and Beerappa are expert sheep-breeders. The family is depicted as under the overall supervision of Akkamankali, and that gives us a clue that the Yadava families were still under the influence of the matriarchal system. Beerappa had a maternal uncle who had a young daughter, Kamarathi. Beerappa loved Kamarathi and wanted to marry her, but his uncle did not intend to give his daughter to Beerappa because he was a poor orphan. Beerappa's family had only a few sheep whereas his uncle had a big herd of sheep. However, Beerappa was firm in the resolve that he would marry his *mardalu* (uncle's daughter), Kamarathi. He waited till his herd grew and he himself acquired the strength to defeat his uncle and marry Kamarathi. His sister kept on requesting him to give up the idea because their uncle was a wicked man and it would be difficult to win him over. But Beerappa was adamant.

One day Beerappa convinced his sister, took her permission and went to his uncle's village. There he met Kamarathi and they planned to elope. On learning of this, his uncle mobilized his forces and confronted Beerappa. But Beerappa defeated his uncle and reached his home along with his beloved. Akkamankali performed their marriage with the involvement of the people in his caste and also the other villagers.

The story has several scenes that pertain separately to Akkamankali, Beerappa and Kamarathi. We see Akkamankali dealing with the problems of feeding the sheep, shearing the wool and milking them in the absence of her brother. The narrative indicates that Mankali was capable of handling all the activities related to sheep and goat-rearing. In the story, the male and female domains are not treated as separate. The unmarried Akkamankali's place in Beerappa's house is the exact opposite of the Brahmin widow Buchamma's place in the Brahmin household in Gurjada Appa Rao's novel *Kanyashulkam;* it is also the opposite of Lakshmi, Sita or Saraswathi's place in the Hindu brahminical narratives. Nowhere in the story does Beerappa insult or chide his sister simply because she remained unmarried, nor does she live as a dependent, helpless woman. At every key turn of the narrative, Akkamankali plays an important role. At every major step Beerappa consults his sister.

The entire story revolves around preserving the idea of marriage based on love, reinforcing man-woman equality and developing sheep-breeding as an occupation.

What do all these Dalitbahujan Goddess/God images, roles, narratives signify? The cultural, economic and political ethos of these Goddesses/Gods is entirely different from Hindu hegemonic Gods and Goddesses. The Dalitbahujan Goddesses/Gods are culturally rooted in production, protection and procreation. They do not distinguish between one section of society and the other, one caste and the other. In these stories there is no scope for creation of an enemy image. War and violence are not at all central to the philosophical notions of the people. Ritualism is a simple activity which does not involve economic waste. Despite there being such a strong sense of the sacred, Dalitbahujan society never allowed the emergence of a priestly class/caste that is alienated from production and alienates the Goddesses and Gods from the people. There is little or no distance between the Gods and Goddesses and the people. In fact the people hardly depend on these Goddesses/ Gods. To whatever extent it exists, and contact is needed, the route between the deity and people is direct. Barriers like language, sloka or mantra are not erected.

How do Hindu Gods and Goddesses compare with Dalitbahujan's Goddesses/Gods? The Hindu Gods are basically war heroes and mostly from wars conducted against Dalitbahujans in order to create a society where exploitation and inequality are part of the very structure that creates and maintains the caste system. The Hindus have a male-centered mythology and women are restricted to gender-specific roles and rendered sexual objects. Though the brahminical Hindus claim that their tradition is rooted in non-violence, the truth is the other way round. All the Hindu Gods were propagators of violent wars. Their dharma is a caste dharma and their living styles, rich and exploitative. Production is made their first enemy. The fact that these Gods are approachable only through a priest and can understand only Sanskrit is enough indication that their alienation from the people is total.

The Dalitbahujans' Goddesses/Gods tradition is the exact opposite in every respect. It is time that we confront these differences and understand them. It is important that scholars from the Dalitbahujan tradition enter into a debate with brahminical scholars in a big way. These brahminical scholars and leaders who talk about Hindutva being the religion of all castes must realize that the Scheduled Castes, Other Backward Classes, and Scheduled Tribes of this country have nothing in common with the Hindus. For centuries, even when Dalitbahujans tried to unite all castes, the Brahmins, the Baniyas and the Kshatriyas opposed the effort. Even today, no Brahmin adopts the names of our Goddesses/Gods; even today, they do not understand that the Dalitbahujans have a much more humane and egalitarian tradition and culture than the Hindu tradition and culture. Even today, our cultural tradition is being treated as meritless. If the Brahmins, the Baniyas, the Kshatriyas and the neo-Kshatriyas of this country want unity among diversity, they should join us and look to Dalitization, not Hinduization.

CHAPTER 6

Hindu Death and Our Death

The way human beings are born is the same except for the fact that the mother who gives birth suffers less or more according to her caste/class background. Our birth into a particular caste is accidental. We may have little control over our upbringing in caste-culture. After a certain age we continue to live in the culture of our own caste through a conscious decision. Having been born into a caste, very few—we can count them on our fingers—consciously move out of their caste-culture.

Though it is not in our hands to decide where we should be born, it is certainly in our own hands to decide how we should die. It is a fact that death is inevitable, but it is also a fact that such death can be moulded into a death according to our own ideas and beliefs. In the concept of death, and the experience of death, Dalitbahujans and Hindus differ in a big way. In our country there is Dalitbahujan death and there is Hindu—Brahmin, Baniya, Kshatriya and neo-Kshatriya—death. Thus, the notion of death differs between Hindus and Dalitbahujans more than it differs between people who belong to two different religions, say, Islam and Christianity.

HINDU BRAHMINICAL DEATH

The difference between Hindu brahminical death and Dalitbahujan death lies in the very concept of death itself. What is the Brahmin's notion of life and death? A Brahmin believes that life must be lived for the sake of death which will make him eternal. To live this way is to live a life that constantly thinks about death. Life in this universe must ensure a perennial life in the other world, that is, in heaven. The Gods that he/she propitiates, time and again are to provide two things. One, a happy life here on this earth, which in philosophical terms is a *kshanabhanguram* (a life that survives only a minute). At the same time, however, this short span on this earth must also be made to ensure a permanent life of privilege and pleasure. So, for a Hindu, death is a transition from this kshanabhanguram to eternity. But how does one spend this very short life here? One should eat in the name of that God who guarantees a permanent happy life. One should eat all the best things available on this earth to please the God who bestows the life of permanence. Though this body merely awaits day in and day out the transitory death that will carry it from the kshanabhanguram to eternity, it must eat rice, dal, milk, vegetables, ghee, fruit and nuts in various forms. It must eat all this in the form of *daddoojanam, pulihoora, perugannam* (these are names of different varieties of rice foods), *pappu kuuralu,* and other curries, in several flavours. Some curries must be sour; some must be sweet; ghee plays an important role in the cuisine. The vessel holding ghee has a special place in this impermanent life. All this must be followed by sweets—laddus, jileebis, fruit salad, and so on. In the sweets too, those made of ghee occupy the highest place. In other words the kshanabhanguram body ought to be as fat as possible, with a rounded belly and unexercised muscles.

In this impermanent life, sex also plays an important role. To the Gods who enjoy the pleasures of the other world the most beautiful women like Ramba, Urvashi, Tilothama and Menaka were available. In order to facilitate this life of kshanabhanguram, of few pleasures, and to ensure a permanent life where more and more pleasures will be available, a son is indispensable. Since it is essential to ensure that the son is his and his alone, he needs a wife who enters his life when she is a child who has not yet attained puberty, and who will later produce a son. When a Brahmin died, if not now, in the past, to ensure his permanent pleasure in heaven, his wife must also die along with him and make herself into a sati.

In the process of working for this most-needed death, two things are necessary: *(i)* leisure and *(ii)* prayer. Leisure in this context is a divine leisure. It must keep the mind focussed on acquiring the permanent life and partaking the pleasures thereof. However, this leisure is also used to develop skills that negate the Others (who are sinners because they produce the goods and commodities that prolong the life of kshanabhanguram that a Brahmin would like to end as soon as possible). Why should he eat the products produced by the labour power of Dalitbahujan castes which will prolong his life on this earth? He believes he is eating not for his own sake but eating for God who alone can ensure him moksha, or release from worldly life. Why should he indulge in sex which only results in another life, like his own, which he himself wants to end? Even this he does for the sake of God's eternity which in turn becomes his own eternity. As I said earlier, a son is essential if he is to enter heaven, and this son is a gift of God, who is also eager to take this *punyaatma* (one who has done only good by not working at all) back to his kingdom. Why is the Brahmin a punyaatma? Because he has eaten all that is produced by the Dalitbahujans and also treated all of them as untouchable rascals. Thus, for a Brahmin, that is, for a Hindu, food and sex are two prerequisites of death.

The life of leisure when supplied with food and sex, automatically ensures two things. One, it ensures that the kshanabhanguram is longer than the unsanctified life of the Dalitbahujans because it gets the best of foods. The emphasis on sex ensures the continuance of this life in his progeny. But this truth is systematically glossed over with the second instrument—prayer. Prayer provides legitimacy for all this drama. Prayer is a weapon in the hands of a Brahmin. It sets him apart from the rest of the masses. It is through this prayer that he establishes his hold over the rest of society. In a fit of madness, which might be a result of their lifetime alienation from work, life itself begins to look meaningless to them. They call this madness the life of penance.

However, when a Brahmin, who does penance throughout his life and who fathers a son to ensure a place in heaven, dies, according to the brahminical notion, it is the day when God's call comes. This death appears very different from the death of a Dalitbahujan. A

Brahmin's death is adjusted with the movement of stars, *grahas* (planets), and so on. Death is not supposed to be mourned. Immediately after the death of a person, the Brahmins around pour into the house. Some begin pujas, some begin *prardhanas,* some begin bhajans. The people around are not allowed to weep loudly; they can only do so quietly. After the dead body is carried out, only men follow the funeral procession. Women are not allowed to take part.

From the day a Brahmin dies till the twelfth day, instead of mourning, feasting takes place. While alive the Brahmin's body is sacred (this is the reason why others must not touch him except when doing *paadapuja,* that is, touching the feet and asking for his blessing). After death that sacred soul begins its voyage to *swarga* and the body becomes untouchable (this notion got extended to Dalitbahujans also). The priests pray for their fellow priest's soul to be given a permanent seat in the other world. Even the death of a Brahmin is a tax on the already burdened Dalitbahujans. The living Brahmins will have more feasts, which in turn will result in their extracting from the Dalitbahujan masses. In the beginning, there is a *shraaddha* every day, gradually it becomes a month-wise shraaddha, and afterwards every year at the death anniversary a shraaddha takes place. Even after death the soul does not merge into collectivity.

Is there any change in these notions of life and death among modern Brahmins? Not qualitatively. There are perhaps some quantitative changes, but the essence remains the same. Even today, an average urban Brahmin does not think differently from his ancestors. In post-colonial India, the Brahmins have urbanized themselves in a big way. The notion of swarga may not dominate their day-to-day life. There might be slight reversals in their notions of this life and the life after death. Because of fast growing technology, an average Brahmin or Baniya publicly confesses that the life here should be lived with all the luxuries, but this does not mean that he or she reduces the emphasis on the permanent life in swarga. To achieve this the discourse has been changed from dharma to merit. The state and the civil society are moulded to suit 'merit' in modern times just as it was moulded to suit dharma in ancient times.

Earlier the life of kshanabhanguram involved only eating without producing the food that was eaten. Modern Brahmins and Baniyas not only eat the best and most modern food available in India, but they also have the best houses. Their styles of living have been modernized. They now have cushioned doublebeds, airconditioned houses, air-cooled bedrooms (depending of course on the climate). They have the most decorated houses. Even here modernity has been cleverly brahminized. The centrepiece in a well-decorated room is not uncommonly a painting of a Hindu God or Goddess. A picture that is commonly found in the homes of brahminical families is that of Krishna's *radhasaaradhyam* (as charioteer); another popular image is that of Krishna preaching the Gita to Arjuna. All this is now couched as art and stamped with the stamp of modernity. The largest number of colour TVs are possessed by Brahmin and Baniya families. The largest number of private cars (perhaps about 70 percent) belong to Brahmins and Baniyas. The largest number of people who travel by air in India are Brahmins and Baniyas. The highest number of people who travel in airconditioned trains and luxury buses are again Brahmins and Baniyas. Today they do all this in the name of service to the 'masses'. They did the same thing in ancient India, calling it the service of God, done in the interest of *loka kalyaanam*. Nationalism reformulated brahminical philosophy, replacing the divine with the 'masses', as this was essential at a time when adultfranchise was on the global agenda. The change from 'God' to 'masses' is a trick of the trade. Expanding the scope of the pleasures to be enjoyed in this world, pleasures that are increasingly on sale in a capitalist market, is an essential prerequisite, and hence the restructuring of Brahminism is the need of the day. During the post-1947 period, enjoying political power became one of the pleasures of life.

This did not diminish, however, the Hindu ambition for the permanency of life in the other world. As the Brahmins and the Baniyas exploit the Dalitbahujans from positions of political and bureaucratic power and industrial and capital markets, there is a growing sense of sin which, in their view, may bring early death. There is a danger that after death the sin may haunt them in the other world too. This is sought to be overcome by constructing posh temples and establishing puja rooms in their modern houses. Both in the temples and in the puja rooms of posh houses, brahminical gods—Rama, Krishna, Shiva, Ganapathi, Lakshmi, Parvathi, and so on, are depicted in modern forms. All this is to facilitate exploitation and also to prolong life here and in the other world.

Even in modern times death is mourned with feasting and feeding people from their own castes. After death, the third day celebrations, the eleventh day celebrations, month celebrations, anniversary celebrations, all are occasions for feasting. Those who have done little except cheating and eating in their lifetimes are made to be historically important persons. Their biographies are written, their photographs are publicized and their names appear in the media. Newspaper advertisements have become modern methods of 'upper' caste celebrations of a person's death, and of the perpetuation of the dead man's memory. They have acquired crores to spend in this way. Even after a Hindu dies, living Hindus go on wasting social wealth on him. Obviously, they think this social wealth is their (Hindu) wealth.

THE DALITBAHUJAN DEATH

For Dalitbahujans life now and life after death has a different meaning from that of the Hindus. For them, life is a one-time affair. This philosophy is expressed in the proverb, *puttindokasaare sachindokasaare* ('we are born only once and die only once'). A dead man/woman in a Dalitbahujan family is a loss in terms of productive work. Each person would have developed several productive skills of his/her own. Each person would have added some instruments for enhancing production. A Kurumaa man would have discovered new areas of sheep-breeding. He would have improved the skills of cutting wool. A Kurumaa woman would have added to the skills of spinnning wool. Several women spun wool, rolling the spinning stick on their thigh muscles. If a woman who discovered the technique of wool spinning died in the process of discovery and in the process of putting it to use, sometimes the process stopped for generations. In the death of such a woman the development of technology stagnated for quite some time.

In this philosophy there is no concept of heaven or swarga. All the descriptions of swarga that are part of the day-to-day discourses of Hindu families do not exist in Dalitbahujan families. In a Dalitbahujan view, life here must be lived for life's sake. Further, life here is related to work. The more it works, the more sacred that life becomes. The proverbs, *panee praardhana* ('work is worship'), *panileeni paapi* ('one who does not work is a sinner') demonstrate that work alone makes life meaningful. In contrast to brahminical notions of eating, Dalitbahujans consider eating as a part of life on earth itself. Dalitbahujan women demonstrate this philosophy in which eating is considered as a part of work. They say *anni panulu tiirinaayi, okka tinee pani tappa* ('all my work is done; the only job left is to eat'). The routine process of eating has no relationship to God or to the sacred. As I have discussed in Chapters 1 and 2, both cooking and eating are done at a secular and mundane level.

Among the Dalitbahujans, quite a considerable debate takes place about whether human beings have to eat to live or whether they should live to eat. In their discourses they normally come to the conclusion that they have to eat to live. As work is central to their lives, every discourse relates to work. The context itself provides answers to their philosophical questions. The life of the Dalitbahujans starts with work but does not start with bed-coffee or bed-tea. It starts with cleaning: sweeping the surroundings, washing, taking the cattle to the field, tilling the land, and so on. In their everyday lives, the question of eating comes much later. A Kurumaa's life starts straightaway, attending to the herd of sheep or entering into the field, a Goudaa starts his day by reaching the toddy tree, a Maadigaa starts his day by taking his *aare* (an instrument that cuts skin) into his hands, working at his household industry of shoe-making. Usually they do not wash their faces in the morning. Face-washing and cleaning the teeth takes place at *buvva yalla* (food eating time, around 10 a.m.). The conclusion that they have to 'eat to live' is based on their daily experience: they work first, eat later.

The act of eating is very simple. A woman quickly swallows some rice from the *buvva kunda* (rice pot) and some curry from the *kuura kanchudu* (curry bowl). She also feeds her children with the same food and carries some to her husband. The husband stops his work for a few minutes, eats his food and resumes the work. Based on this daily practice, they conclude that they have to eat to live. This philosophy of eating to live is exactly the opposite of the brahminical notions of living to eat. The Gods and the Goddesses whom they worship occasionally—Pochamma, Maisamma, Potaraju—do not appear to be Gods or Goddesses who order them to make obeisance in daily puja; they do not demand divine feasting. Even on festive occasions, eating does not involve even one-tenth of the ritual that the Hindu brahminical Gods and Goddesses require. So, the number of items of food that appear in the ritual only indicate the desire of human beings to eat those things.

At a festival, the Dalitbahujans will kill a lamb, a goat or a hen and give a small amount (padi) to the Goddess or the God once in a while, but life in terms of the prosperity or death in terms of eternity does not figure in their relationship with that Goddess or God. Fear is not totally absent, but fear is not given a philosophical justification. Further, 'freedom from fear' does not require the eternal protection of the Goddess or the God. In other words, the notion of prayer as investment in eternal life is not the basis of the relationship between the Goddesses or Gods and the human beings. One reason for this could be that among the Dalitbahujans, of the two things that a Hindu expects as a matter of right—leisure and prayer—are absent.

The interaction of Dalitbahujans with the land, water, forests, animals and reptiles is in order to get something new out of these things. It is a scientific interaction and a creative one. This is the reason why in their day-to-day lives the earth is referred to as Mother Earth *(talli bhoodeevi)*, the forest is referred to as Mother Forest *(adavi talli)*, the water is referred to as Mother Ganga *(Gangamma talli)*. None of these forces demand prayer; they are forces that the Dalitbahujans constantly interact with. If any of these notions exists among Hindus, it is because of the influence of Dalitization. It is through the interaction with natural forces that the new emerges, and this newness through the addition of labour (not leisure) changes into a socially useful product. A Hindu uses every one of these socially useful products, but does not know how, or by which process, it is produced. He or she thinks that it is a product of prayer. The Dalitbahujans know that it is a product of labour. Therefore, here labour is valued and leisure is condemned.

Since this labour is combined with constant interaction with other social beings, it produces a language, a grammar and a literature, for example, a song is an integral part of labour. If any Dalitbahujan is not involved in work, such a person is known as *paniipaata leenoodu* (a person without work or song). The parallel proverb of brahminical Hindus is *chaduvu sandhya leenoodu* (a person without education or prayer). In the Dalitbahujan notion of panii paata, we find creativity and science; in the brahminical notion of chaduvu sandhya, education has degenerated into a non-labouring leisure activity, which causes human beings to degenerate. Dalitbahujan philosophy is not linked to the sacred. The reason for the degeneration of Hindu society, even in the modern period, lies here. Leisure and prayer are concepts that not only have different connotations in Dalitbahujan lives, they have a very marginal role in their socio-political formation.

What does sex mean to Dalitbahujans? Sex in these lives is not an activity of leisure-based pleasure but an essential social function. This does not mean pleasure is seen as antithetical, but the brahminical leisure-based pleasure does not find any justification. A people who developed so many arts, never thought of developing, as Vatsyayana did, the arts of sexuality. For them such sexuality has leisure-based vulgarity and it had no scope of acquiring a social base. That is the reason why the Vatsyayana-type of exercise is absent even in the oral tradition of Dalitbahujans. For example, while the brahminical temples are full of sculptures based on Vatsyayana's sixty-four arts, no Dalitbahujan temple—no shrine of Pochamma, Maisamma, Kaatamaraju, Beerappa—bears such decorations.

As against a brahminical notion of sex, the Dalitbahujans perceive the man-woman pairing as a social combination of collective production and collective procreation. Procreating children is a social function and also adds hands to the labouring process. It is not that a son does not get better treatment than a daughter, and not that a son does not play a ritual role when the father or the mother dies. *Talagooru,* a water pot carried in front of a dead body, does play a role at the time of death. But a son is essentially seen as the caretaker of old parents, not as one who ensures a place in heaven. As the notion of swarga is not central, life after death is not important. If a person lives a socially useful life, it acquires meaning. Death is an end in itself. If someone plays a socially negative role, after death such a person becomes a devil and keeps hanging around troubling others. Thus the difference between *punyam* and *paapam* is that punyam ends life forever, while paapam turns a person into a devil. Dalitbahujan castes perform third day and eleventh day ceremonies, but after that the dead people lose their identity. Anniversaries are not celebrated and the identity of the dead person is not retained. All the dead become part of the *peddalu* (elders who have passed away). The priest, though he comes and performs the shraaddha, never—even notionally—concedes an equal place for Dalitbahujans. No priest proclaims that in performing the shraaddha for the Dalitbahujan, his or her right to enter swarga is recognized. In fact, even the death of a Dalitbahujan is a means used by the priests to make money. In the modern urban areas, Dalitbahujans do not touch a dead body. This is because their reference point has become the Brahmin family. They have internalized Brahminism.

Hindu and Dalitbahujan concepts of the death of women also differ. A Hindu woman does not find any important place in Hindu ritual hierarchy. A woman's death is mourned, but not eloquently. Among 'upper' castes, when a woman dies if a man weeps loudly, such a man is said to be unmanly. But among the Dalitbahujans, weeping aloud is possible. People gather around the dead body, and generally the women outnumber the men. I remember when my mother died, my father wept. The men around began to say, 'You are a man, how can you cry like that?' But the women intervened and said, 'Let him cry, if he does not cry now when will he cry?'

It is this autonomous space and public role of women that sets the norm for man-woman relations among the Dalitbahujan castes on a different footing even at the time of death. They provide a different social space for the death of Dalitbahujan women.

After death, in the case of women too, the third day, eleventh day and the completion of one month, are observed as *Maashikam* (death ritual). After that, the dead person is only another of the dead elders. Among Dalitbahujans, the bodies of married men and women are burnt down to ashes. Children and unmarried women or single men of whatever age are buried. This practice is an extension of Brahmin practice. Cremation is an unscientific method of dealing with dead bodies because it leaves no history in the form of fossils. If the whole world had done what the Brahmin rituals require, the whole fossil history of human bodies would not have been available. Quite a lot of ancient and medieval history was reconstructed based on skeletons of the human bodies that could be studied even after centuries. Burning of human bodies burns every evidence. I wish the Dalitbahujans could have developed a different practice even in this respect by giving up the practice of burning dead bodies. Today the practice of burning dead bodies is used by state agencies like the police and the army to destroy the evidence of torture and murder. Brahminism must have evolved this practice in ancient India as the Hindus killed several Dalitbahujans who had revolted against them to destroy evidence of torture and murder.

Dalitbahujans are not used to being photographed, the old especially offer resistance. This is because the Brahmins did not allow them to maintain any history. Though architecture, painting and sculpture were Dalitbahujan occupations, a painter or an artist never left a history or a picture of his or her family. Ironically, it was the Dalitbahujans who painted and sculpted the family histories of the Brahmins and the Kshatriyas. But they were not allowed to retain a sense of their past in any visible form. This is another reason why the death of a Dalitbahujan means that he or she dies for ever. But now we must change this situation. We must see that the dead Dalitbahujans would live in the form of history; that they live in art, in paintings, in sculpture and in literature.

Hinduism left no stone unturned to destroy the wisdom, the faith, the feelings, and the images of the Dalitbahujans while they were living and also after their death. In this respect Hindu Brahminism is unparalled. Its inhumanity is unequalled. As I have shown, while living the Dalitbahujans share nothing with Hindus and even after death they share nothing with them.

We should change this relationship not by Hinduizing ourselves. We must change this relationship by dalitizing the brahminical forces. Throughout Indian history the Dalitbahujans have been the thesis and the brahminical forces the anti-thesis. The relationship between these forces in the form of thesis and anti-thesis has resulted in producing a synthesis but it is a mutilated synthesis. It is unnatural for a section of human beings to acquire the role of anti-thesis and continue to play that role always. It is realistic and natural that all human beings become thesis and confront nature as their anti-thesis. This is essential if the relationship between Indians as human beings is to acquire a positive homogeneity with plurality, and not a negative homogeneity which will destroy plurality itself.

CHAPTER 7

Dalitization Not Hinduization

As I have argued in the preceding chapters, the life-world of the Dalitbahujans of India has hardly anything in common with the socio-cultural and political environment of Hindu-Brahminism. The Dalitbahujans live together with the Hindus in the civil society of Indian villages and urban centres, but the two cultural worlds are not merely different, they are opposed to each other. Hindu thinking is set against the interests of Dalitbahujan castes; Hindu mythology is built by destroying the Dalitbahujan cultural ethos. Dalitbahujan castes were never allowed to develop into modernity and equality. The violent, hegemonic, brahminical culture sought to destroy Dalitbahujan productive structures, culture, economy and its positive political institutions. Everything was attacked and undermined. This process continues in post-Independence India.

While conducting the anti-colonial struggle, brahminical leaders and ideologues did not attempt to build an anti-caste egalitarian ideology. On the contrary, they glorified brutal Hindu institutions. They built an ideology that helped brahminical forces reestablish their full control which had, to some extent, been weakened during the political rule of the Mughals and the British. In the building of brahminical nationalism, Raja Rammohan Roy, at one stage, and Gandhi, at another, played key roles in recreating 'upper' caste hegemony. After 1947, in the name of democracy, the Brahmins, the Baniyas and the neo-Kshatriyas have come to power. Post-colonial development in its entirety has been systematically cornered by these forces. The Brahmins have focussed their attention on politico-bureaucratic power, the Baniyas established their hegemony on capitalist markets and the Neo-Kshatriyas established their control over the agrarian economy. This modern triumvirate restructured the state and society to affirm and reproduce their hegemonic control.

In spite of the immense hold of modern Brahminism on various structures of power, the intellectual forces that emerged from the womb of the Dalitbahujan social structure as a result of both education and reservations have attempted to fracture modern Brahminism in many ways. The elite of modern Brahminism recognized this force and resurrected Brahminism in the more aggressive form of Hindutva in the anti-Mandal ideologies, the Ayodhya-based Rama slogan, as well as in the Sangh Parivar's theory of 'Akhandabharat' and 'minority appeasement'. All these are part of the anti-Dalitbahujan package.

Such a basically anti-Dalitbahujan thesis is advanced to modernize classical Hindu *varnadharma* to suit post-colonial capitalist structures, so that Hinduism itself can modernize in a way that will sustain the hegemony of brahminical forces. This is the reason why the thesis is put forward that Hinduization should be within the broad framework of urbanization, modernization, and so on. We reject the Hinduization programme in toto for two reasons. One, Hinduism has never been a humane philosophy. It is the most brutal religious school that the history of religions has witnessed. The Dalitbahujan castes of India are the living evidence of its brutality. Second, even if Hinduization expresses a desire to humanize itself in future, there is no scope for this to happen, since the history of religion itself is coming to an end. We must, therefore, dalitize our entire society as Dalitization will establish a new egalitarian future for Indian society as a whole.

WHAT IS DALITIZATION?

Dalitization requires that the whole of Indian society learns from the *Dalitwaadas* (here I am speaking specifically about Scheduled Caste localities). It requires that we look at the Dalitwaadas in order to acquire a new consciousness. It requires that we attend to life in these waadas; that we appreciate what is positive, what is humane and what can be extended from Dalitwaadas to the whole society.

It is common sense knowledge that the starting point of Dalitbahujan society is the collective of 'untouchable' houses, the homesteads of the Maadigaas and Maalaas (similar castes exist in almost all linguistic regions of India). What is most striking about Maadigaa and Maalaa society is its collective living and collective consciousness. The human being in the Dalitwaadas is not only a collective being but also a secular social being. Here human relationships operate in a mode that has been sensitised to human needs. Though Dalitbahujan society does have contradictions, these contradictions are not antagonistic. They are friendly and can be resolved. Their social context is productive and distributive. Equality is its innate strength. In the current repressive social structure of the village, it is only the Dalitbahujan masses who have had the strength to survive as productive beings. Consciousness in the Dalitwaada is not individual but collective. Human beings relate to each other basically on humane terms. The material basis of the society is rooted not in wealth but in labour power. However Dalitbahujan labour power earns diminishing returns. Such diminishing returns have the effect of completely alienating them. In fact, there is a triple process of alienation taking place in the Dalitwaadas: *(i)* They are alienated from village production and marketing; *(ii)* they are alienated from the main village social setting; and *(iii)* they are alienated from themselves. In this respect, the Dalitbahujans of India live in far more adverse conditions than the working classes in the West. Yet the hope of life among them is greater and stronger. Where does this hope come from? This hope comes from their own inner strength that expresses itself in the form of Dalitbahujan culture and consciousness. Its soul lies in its collective consciousness.

In the Dalitwaada the individual is subsumed into the collectivity. While being a member of that collectivity, this individual retains a certain individuality. The interaction with nature on a day-to-day basis reproduces the freshness of life. To ensure that life within the Dalitwaada is not free, within every village the 'upper' castes, particularly the Brahmins and the Baniyas, have created mini-states that constantly oppress the Dalitbahujans both physically and spiritually. Despite all this Dalitbahujans have been re-energizing themselves to struggle to improve their lives. This is possible because of their collective consciousness.

What are the implications of Dalitbahujan collective consciousness? Everything—good or bad—that takes place within the Dalitwaada is shared by everyone. Pleasure, pain and social events are all shared. If there is a birth in one house, both the pleasures and the pains of that birth are also social. The mother's labour pains are at least emotionally shared by all the womenfolk of the Dalitwaada. The pleasure of giving birth to a new human being, who will add to the number of working hands, a human being who is never regarded as a burden on society, this pleasure is not merely that of the mother and the father but of the whole waada. If there is a death, the whole Dalitwaada shares in it emotionally. Men and women are both part of the funeral procession, cremation or burial. All the women and the men gather to mourn the loss of a human being who had been part of their labour collective; a human being who ate with them, drank with them and smoked with them; a human being who was never a burden as long as that person was able-bodied. It is commonly observed by the villagers that Dalitbahujan women and men go to every house where death has taken place—even to the 'upper' caste houses. There they recount as they mourn, the 'good' that the person has done. On this occasion, they do not mention shortcomings or evil deeds. But in the normal course of life the defects of 'upper' castes occupy the principal place in their discourse.

Very recently I happened to visit a village where a rich Reddy's only son (aged twenty) had committed suicide, ostensibly because his stingy father had refused to spend money on his education. The first people to reach the Reddy's house to abuse the stingy father were the Maadigaas of the village. They abused the father and mourned for the boy. The response of the other Dalitbahujans, by and large, was the same, whereas the 'upper' castes 'understood' the father-son relations of that family within the context of private property. The so-called upper castes saw what was 'wrong' in the boy's anger against his property-conscious father. A father who was ultimately accumulating property in the interest of the lone son. The Dalitbahujan understanding of the father-son relationship was the opposite of that of the 'upper' castes. For them the question was totally different. They posed the question as follows: Is property meant for human beings, or human beings meant for property? To appreciate the implications of this question we must understand the whole notion of private property among the Dalitbahujan masses.

DALITBAHUJAN NOTION OF PRIVATE PROPERTY

The Maalaa-Maadigaa society has not become a society structured by private property. The notion of private property has not become part of their thinking in any major way. Individuality and possession of property has not acquired the pride of place in Dalitbahujan consciousness that it has in Hindu consciousness. If Dalitbahujans get hold of a goat or a sheep or a bull or a cow they share the meat. Even today, they do not weigh the meat first but simply distribute it by dividing it into equal shares, one share for each family. Such distribution has become central to the Dalitbahujan consciousness. Even the welfare doles that the government gives are shared equally. This is one of the main reasons why welfare inputs disappear into collective consumption within no time.

Why is it that they do not acquire the consciousness of retaining something for tomorrow, for two days, for two months or for two years, thus forming private property of their own? The main reason for not acquiring such private property is rooted in the confidence they have in their power to labour. Dalitbahujans are the most hard-working people in village society. For them it is their labour power that is property. If the Dalitwaadas had disengaged themselves from the labour process, the village economies would have collapsed long ago. The Dalitwaada knows that for the labour that they invest in the production—whether agrarian or non-agrarian—very little comes back to them. Every day they consume something less than what they need to re-energize themselves. Thus, they know that every day they are also being alienated from their own selves. Yet they are not disillusioned about life. They take life as a struggle in both production and procreation. Far from being a burden to the society, they are the productive pillars that keep the whole society standing, the blood that keeps the whole society alive.

In contrast to this, the 'upper' castes are the most non-productive and lazy forces. Their values have been completely distorted by their life of perennial luxury. Their notion of private property is inhuman and exploitative. They can live tomorrow only on the property they preserve and to acquire that property, any brutality can be committed and it can be regarded as part of Hindu dharma. Among the brahminical forces there is no notion of 'work'. Labour is negated. All relations among human beings are reduced to relations of private property and distrust. Human values stand destroyed to the core. Eating and sleeping become the two principal tasks of human beings. Not that all Brahmin-Baniyas are rich. There are poor among them. Even they do not make their living by manual work (small pockets like Uttarakhand are exceptions).

Dalitbahujans, on the other hand, layer by layer, keep working for the well-being of these so-called upper castes. Clearly what needs to be changed is the culture of 'upper' castes who live by exploiting Dalitbahujan labour and by converting the fruits of that labour into their property. All human beings including the Brahmins and the Baniyas must learn to live with the kind of confidence that the Dalitbahujans have. What is that confidence? The confidence that 'our tomorrow is guaranteed by our labour'. That is possible only when they begin to think in terms of the Dalitization of brahminical society.

As a result of brahminical alienation from productive work, Hindu society has created a very powerful notion of private property. The non-productive life of the 'upper' castes can survive only on private property. Unlike in non-caste systems, the accumulation of private property by brahminical Hinduism did not come about through a mixture of labour, investment and exploitation. The caste system has given enormous scope for accumulation of private property with a single instrument: exploitation. The spiritual mantra alone was brahminical investment. The whole world knows about the

Brahmins' fear of labour and their disgust for work. Brahminical greed and gluttony ensure that property is accumulated only through exploitation. Moreover, property accumulated through such exploitation is given the highest social status. Brahminical literature concerns only the rich. Brahminical Hindu society has assigned all virtues to the rich and all vices to the poor. As far as I know, this is not true of the priesthood of other religions. The foundations of 'upper' caste culture lies in this brahminical notion of private property and non-productive living. Accumulation of property is designed to enable people to live without working. In Hindu society private property is not a social reserve to be used when society as a whole needs it. This is one place where Gandhi was wrong. For Brahmins, all that is in their possession becomes sacred, and is untouchable by others. If a Brahmin has some extra rice, it will not be given away. Even Baniya property is sacred property. The casteization of property destroys the social basis of property. In fact, it is because of the caste system, which in turn casteized property, that the system of property could not play a progressive role in India at any stage.

LABOUR AS LIFE

For Dalitbahujans labour is life. For a Dalitbahujan body, labour is as habitual as eating is to the stomach. In fact, every Dalitbahujan body produces more than it consumes. As a result, Dalitbahujan life recreates itself in labour more than it recreates itself through eating and drinking. While labouring, a Dalitbahujan mind does not disengage from thinking but goes on producing ideas that make labour a pleasure. If labour is not pleasure, if Dalitbahujan minds do not derive pleasure out of that labouring process, given the low levels of consumption on which they subsist, Dalitbahujan bodies would have died much earlier than they do. Even if Dalitbahujans were to consider work as a monotonous, tortuous course of life, given the amount of labour that they expend during their lifetimes, death would have invited them much earlier than it does today.

If without giving up such a practice of labouring, and labouring with pleasure, when adequate calories of food are provided, a

Dalitbahujan body will live longer and more healthily than the non-labouring 'upper' caste/class body.

In the process of labour Dalitbahujans engage in a constant intercourse with the land. Their thorough understanding of land and its producitivity, its colour and combination, is solely responsible for increase in productivity. Even before 'knowledge from without' (what we call urban-based, expert knowledge) influenced Dalitbahujan productive skills, they had been experimenting constantly to improve their labour productivity, trying to understand scientifically the relationship between land and seed. They also tried to understand the relationship between the seed and human biological systems. Before cross-breeding was studied in modern laboratories, the Dalitbahujans had cross-bred seed systems. Dalitbahujan women selected and preserved seeds for planting. They maintained huge stores of plant genes. They grafted plants and worked out whole systems of hybridization. All this knowledge was a product of their labour and its creative intercourse with land and nature.

Dalitbahujan labour has creatively interacted with a whole range of non-agrarian plant systems. Dalitbahujans who were engaged in sheep-, goat- and cattle-breeding made tireless investigations of plants and their medicinal values. These investigations were done with an exemplary combination of physical labour and mental acumen. Dalitbahujan knowledge never separated physical labour from mental labour. In India this bifurcation took place in a caste/class form. For Dalitbahujans, physical and mental labour was an integrated whole. If we want to understand the process by which the contradiction between mental and physical labour is resolved as Mao did in the Chinese context, we must return to studying carefully the way the Dalitbahujan societies of India combined mental and physical labour, without a so-called wise man intervening, in the process of labouring to integrate, break open, reintegrate and finally discover new systems. The Dalitbahujan masses have enormous technological and engineering skills which are not divorced from their labour. One who lifts dead cattle also knows the science of skinning it. They themselves know how to process the skin and make chappals, shoes or ropes. All these tasks involve both mental and physical labour. This work is not like reading the Vedas or teaching in a school. Reading the Vedas or teaching in a school does not require much investment of physical labour or creative thought. Certain types of mental labour may not involve physical labour, but all physical labour involves mental labour. Dalitbahujan society has shown exemplary skill in combining both. Take, for example, the Goudaas who climb the toddy trees and combine in themselves the talent of mind and the training of body. While climbing the tree a Goudaa has to exercise his muscle power. He has also to invent ways of climbing tall trees which do not have branches. While climbing, if he does not focus his mind on every step the result is death. A Brahmin dance teacher, while dancing certainly combines both physical and mental labour but does not encounter a risk in every step. Despite this, why is it that brahminical dance has acquired so much value? Why is it that brahminical dance is given so much space in literature? Why not celebrate the beauty and skill of a Goudaa, which over and above being an art, science and an exercise has productive value. As I have already discussed, the tapping of a toddy tree layer by layer, involves enormous knowledge and engaged application besides physical and mental skill. Tapping the gela in a way that makes the toddy but does not hurt the tree, cannot be done by everybody. It needs training and cultivation of mind. Training in this specialization is much more dangerous and difficult than training in reading the Vedas. All the same a Hindu is told to respect and value the training to read Veda mantras, but not the Goudaa skills of producing something which has market-value and consumption-value.

Hindu Brahminism defied all economic theories, including feminist economic theory, that all market-oriented societies valued labour which produced goods and commodities for market consumption. Feminist economic theory points out that though women's labour in the house contributes to the economy, it does not find social respectability or receive economic compensation. In the brahminical economy Dalitbahujan labour (male or female) even if it is produced for market consumption has no value. On the contrary, the so-called mental labour of the Brahmins and the

Baniyas reciting mantras and extracting profit by sitting at the shop desk has been given enormous socioeconomic value. Herein lies the Hindu delegitimization of productive creativity. The brahminical economy even devalued production for the market and privileged its spiritual-mental labour over all other labour processes.

Brahminical scholarship legitimized leisure, mantra, puja, tapasya and soothsaying, though these are not knowledge systems in themselves. Scientific knowledge systems, on the contrary, are available among the Dalitbahujan castes. A pot maker's wholistic approach to knowledge which involves collecting the right type of earth, making it into clay, turning it on the wheel, and firing it requires knowledge of local materials and resources, scientific knowledge of the clay and the firing process, besides a sharp understanding of the market. It requires mental skill to use the fingers, while physically turning the wheel, skill to convert that clay into pots, pitchers and jars—small or big—of all kinds. Firing is an equally skill-intensive process. The oven has to be heated to an exact temperature and the pots baked just long enough for them to become durable and yet retain their attractive colour. This whole scheme is a specialized knowledge in itself. Thus, Kamsalies (goldsmiths) have their own scientific knowledge, Kammaris (blacksmiths) theirs, and Shalaas (weavers) theirs. But all these arts and sciences, all these knowledge systems have been delegitimized. Instead of being given social priority and status, mantric mysticism has been given priority. These knowledge systems will get socioeconomic value only when their legitimacy is established.

Hinduism constructed its own account of Dalitbahujan knowledge systems. As discussed earlier, while the Dalitbahujans live labour as life, the Hindus inverted this principle and privileged leisure over labour. The ancient theoretical formation of the thesis 'leisure as life' was propounded by Vatsyayana in the *Kamasutra,* where he constructs a *nagarika* (citizen) as one who embodies this notion. This very theory was reinstated at different stages of history whenever brahminical Hinduism was in crisis, or whenever Dalitbahujan organic forces rebelled against Hindu theory and practice. As we saw, the 1990 anti-Mandal Hindutva wave again aimed at reviving the 'leisure as life' theory as against the Mandal movement that aimed at universalizing 'labour as life' (irrespective of caste, everyone should do both manual labour and work in an office). In other words, it aimed at dalitizing Indian society. The whole world has overcome the theories of privileging leisure over labour. Whether it is countries like Japan and China or in the West itself, labour has acquired more market value and social status than leisure. Mandalization of the Indian state and society would have integrated us into these universal systems. But Hindu Brahminism reacted to this historical transformation and started the counter-revolutionary Hindutva movement by reemphasizing leisure, mantra and moksha as basic principles which will undermine the onward march of Indian society. But quicker development of Indian society lies in privileging labour over leisure. Only Dalitization of the whole society can achieve this goal.

DALITBAHUJAN DEMOCRACY

Dalitbahujan social systems are democratic in nature, structuring themselves in social collectivity and in a collective consciousness. Collectivity and collective consciousness are reinforced by the negation of the institution of private property. As I have discussed earlier, Dalitbahujan society has negated private property because it has tremendous confidence in its own labour power and because of its concept of labour as life.

In political terms, Dalitbahujan democracy expresses itself in several ways. The relationship between wife and husband, though patriarchal, is also democratic. The wife does not have to be known in her husband's name. She can learn and practise all skills. Human strengths and weaknesses are integrated into Dalitbahujan life. Men and women can abuse each other, at times beat each other, though it is true that often women will be at the receiving end. Between wife and husband, there exists a loving relationship based on shared work that plays a positive role. Though marriages are often arranged and child marriage is practised, divorce and remarriage (*maarumaanam*) are socially accepted. Divorce is made possible for both wife and husband in an open discussion in the Dalitwaada. The caste panchayat, village panchayat and the ammalakkala muchhatlu, women's collectives, all debate the rights and wrongs of the couple and come to a socially acceptable conclusion. Where there is no possibility of continuing to live as a wife and husband, the two may divorce because that is the practical alternative. Of course, the Hindu problem regarding widow-remarriage has never been a problem in Dalitbahujan society. The democracy in the Dalitwaadas is a democracy that works.

The relations between parents and children are far more democratic in Dalitbahujan houses than in Hindu houses. A son or daughter addresses the parents in the familiar singular mode and eats and drinks along with them. There is very little of a hierarchy in the house, waada and caste; vices and virtues are debated more openly in the family, waada and caste than it is in Hindu society. While illiteracy in the Dalitwaadas (illiteracy is imposed on them by the brahminical system) places limitations on their levels of knowledge, the available productive knowledge is freely shared by all. People in the Dalitwaadas live on the basis of equality. We generally do not find huge buildings on the one hand and poor sheds on the other. By and large the whole of the Dalitwaada lives in poverty, but within that poverty there is equality as they all live in similar houses, eat similar food and wear similar clothes. This equality minimizes jealousy and competition among them.

The persistent theory that human beings are by nature, selfish or iniquitous or that the scope for selfishness is removed only when inequality is reduced (as was done in some of the former socialist systems) and its obverse: the theory that human systems do not survive if inequalities are totally removed, both these theories can be disproved by any systematic study of Dalitwaadas, where there is no negative cut-throat competition and no withdrawing into lethargy. There are umpteen examples to show that if there is work for three human days for a person, and a Dalitbahujan is assigned to finish that work, he or she would take two more people along and finish the task in one day—even if it means unemployment for the next two days. This is because of the democratic humanism that the Dalitwaadas are vested with. Amidst poverty there is no dearth of humanity. This is the rich heritage that Dalitwaadas can extend to the whole of Indian society.

In contrast to this, life in the Hindu waadas, particularly the Brahmin or the Baniya households, is marked by selfishness, inequality and cut-throat competition. This is primarily because Hindus are non-productive and anti-labour people. Naturally, therefore, a Hindu family visualizes its survival only in a totally hierarchical and competitive system. This competition is for greater pleasure and 'better' living but even within the same Hindu 'upper' caste they do not appreciate equality. For them equality goes against human nature itself which they regard as thriving on inequality and selfishness. The principle of 'selfishness as natural' has become the philosophical foundation of Hinduism. This was the reason why it could not build a society of internal strength and internal dynamism.

The 'upper' caste political structure is basically authoritarian. Authoritarianism begins within a brahminical home and extends to the rest of civil society. Given the socio-political hegemony of the 'upper' castes, the structures that the brahminical family have evolved are projected to be the structures of Indian society as a whole. Its opposite, that is, Dalitbahujan structures, though they encompass a far larger number of people, indeed the whole working mass of India, is treated by brahminical literary, political and legal texts as nonexistent. As a result, even historians and social scientists from other parts of the world constructed Indian culture and history either in conformity with brahminical theocracy or critiqued it in its own terms without comparing it with the secular and democratic social systems of the Dalitbahujans. If only that had been done, every observer (if not from India, at least from abroad) could have realized that India has always been divided into two cultures and two civilizations: the Dalitbahujan and the brahminical. But this fact has been systematically glossed over.

Dalitbahujan democracy and brahminical authoritarianism express themselves in a conflicting manner in civil society. This conflict is an ongoing process and can be found everywhere. If civil society and the structures of the polity had not been hegemonized by brahminical consent and coercion systems, Dalitbahujan democratic structures would have gained the upper hand and the social system would have been built on the much stronger ethics of production. Indian development would have been set on an entirely different course. The defeat of the Indian systems by colonialists would have become impossible. The resilience of the system would have been thousand times greater. Hinduism is solely responsible for the tragedy of this country.

What is important, however, is that though Hinduism has made every attempt to destroy Dalitbahujan culture and civilization, it has not succeeded. Attempts to provide respectable social status to Dalitbahujan culture and civilization were made by Jyotirao Phule and Ambedkar. As we have seen, the attempts to create a Dalitbahujan hegemony began with the Mandal struggle in 1990. Thus the 1990 Mandal struggle posed several new questions. The forces of democracy, that is, the Dalitbahujans and the minorities, and the forces of brahminical authoritarianism are getting polarized. This polarization places the Dalitization of society on the national agenda.

DALITBAHUJAN MAN–WOMAN RELATIONS

Man-woman relations among Dalitbahujan castes are far more democratic and humane than among the Hindus. This aspect has been examined in some detail in preceding chapters, but it can be usefully reviewed here. Though the institution of patriarchy has its sway over even the Dalitwaadas, a certain degree of freedom for women is guaranteed by inbuilt structures. Since Dalitbahujans do not have property reserves and every individual must therefore work for the family, women are thoroughly integrated into their productive labour system. Not only that, the women are the main driving force of Dalitbahujan society. It is also true that because of the lack of social reserves even young children need to work, which has built a tremendous work ethic among them. All the same it is necessary for the well-being of Dalitbahujan society that these children be provided education. Education is an essential condition of life. As part of this process, both women and men need to be educated.

The important point here is that the skills that Dalitbahujan women have are enormous. They are excellent soil examiners, planters, breeders and selectors of seeds. They have huge stores of medical knowledge. Most of these skills are absolutely lacking among 'upper' caste women. Brahminical society has reduced women to sex objects. The taboo system that was built into Hindu families destroyed their creative abilities. The creativity of these women must be restored. Drawing upon the experiences of Dalitbahujan women is the only way other societies of India can change their course. Similarly, Dalitbahujan men are also productive beings. They have huge reserves of the knowledge of nature. Their knowledge of plants, animals, insects is extremely important for the preservation of the human species. Dalitbahujan men and women's knowledge about soils, seeds, tools and other materials is essential for the growth of science and technology in this country. Without this source knowledge, which forms the core of the knowledge systems, the apex knowledge systems would not have developed.

THE FUTURE

The future is that of Dalitbahujans in India. In order to dalitize society, the Dalitbahujan leadership must know its strengths and weaknesses. The Dalitbahujans of India have suffered hardships all through history. Modern democratic socialist revolutions have now given them some scope to liberate themselves. It is only through their liberation that the rest of the society, namely, the 'upper' castes, can be liberated. But this process can be very painful and tortuous. This was clear from two historic struggles that have taken place so far. The first was the 1990 Mandal struggle and the second was the 1993 Uttar Pradesh elections. In 1990 the Dalitization of the administration was violently resisted. The Janata Dal government was pulled down for the simple reason that it implemented a small section of the Mandal Commission Report. In 1993, after the first Dalitbahujan government was formed at the state level, brahminical forces turned the Uttar Pradesh Assembly into a place of bloody battle. As the house assembled on its first day, 16 December 1993, the brahminical forces of Uttar Pradesh began throwing chappals and missiles at the Dalitbahujan legislators. It was because the brahminical forces now realized that the Dalitbahujan *'raakshas'*, '*mlecchaas*', 'Dravidas' and 'Chandalas' had come to rule. But the Dalitbahujans have shown their determination by retaliating. For the first time in Indian history, as we have read in newspapers and seen on television, the Brahmins have tasted what Dalitbahujan power can be. Perhaps this could be a pointer to the future course of history.

Dalitization of civil society, state and administrative apparatus is not going to be an easy task. The Dalitbahujans want that it should be achieved as peacefully as possible; they have never been lovers of violence. But the enemy forces have survived only through violence. Dalitbahujans have all the sympathies for 'upper' caste women as they have also been victims of Hinduism. But a complex problem arises with the fact that they have been integrated into Brahminism in caste and class terms. Even Brahmin women think that Dalitbahujans are Others.

However, the best way to push Dalitization into 'upper' caste houses, is to address the women. The recent past has shown that the women's movement is receptive to Dalitbahujan questions. They see a parallel in the nature of oppression. Though by and large 'upper' caste women live in better economic/class conditions, at least the most conscious among them will quickly realize the need for Dalitization. Already the 'upper' caste women are choosing Dalitbahujan man-woman relations to brahminical patriarchal relations. They seem to prefer the Dalitbahujan concepts of divorce and remarriage to the wife-murder politics of 'upper' caste families. The educated among them seem to think that the family must be open, as against the wish of 'upper' caste men who feel that the family must be a closed and hidden system.

The attempt to dalitize temples—though that in itself does not have much positive implications in terms of democratizing the system—is being demanded. Brahminical forces are resisting this in a big way. But, whatever it is worth, it is important to capture the Hindu temples by expelling the Brahmins from them as there is a lot of wealth in the temples in the form of gold, silver and land. This wealth has to be seized. At the same time it is important to see that the brahminical God-culture does not get assimilated into Dalitbahujan culture. Dalitbahujans whose consciousness has been brahminized must be made aware of its danger. Productive Dalitbahujan culture should constantly be privileged over Hindu 'swaha' culture. The thousands of existing temples could be converted into public education centres, where the Dalitbahujans begin to reschool the 'upper' castes. This of course will require that they unlearn many things. The task is much more difficult with the Brahmins and the Baniyas than it will be with the neo-Kshatriyas. Yet another major area of Dalitization will be to push the Brahmin-Baniyas into productive work, whether it is rural or urban. Both men and women of the so-called upper castes will resist this with all the strength at their command. This is because among them Hinduism has destroyed all positive elements that normally exist in a human being. During the postcolonial period their energies were diverted to manipulate education, employment, production and development subtly. Their minds are poisoned with the notion that productive work is mean and that productive castes are inferior. No ruling class in the world is as dehumanized as the Indian brahminical castes. They can be rehumanized only by pushing them into productive work and by completely diverting their attention from the temple, the office, power-seeking, and so on.

Even in this respect the neo-Kshatriyas are in a slightly advantageous position. Their roots are still in productive work, but because they are slowly gaining political ascendancy, they are becoming more and more brahminized even in terms of production relations. In socio-political terms they must be first neutralized and then dalitized. Transforming them is not as difficult as transforming the Brahmins and Baniyas since their socio-political roots are within the Dalitbahujan culture.

It must be remembered, however, that the anti-caste revolution in India may take a more tortuous course than even the 'proletarian cultural revolution' did in China. The Brahmins will make it so difficult that even if they are asked to undertake productive work, they will shout from their rooftops that atrocities on the 'intellectuals' are on the increase.

As of today, the Non-Resident Indians (NRIs) belong mostly to the 'upper' castes. The post-capitalist markets into which these NRIs are integrated did not de-caste them. This is very clear from their pro-Hindutva proclamations from abroad. These are the forces that financed Hindutva with dollars. The categorical shift of the Delhi 'intelligentsia' towards Hindutva, as against the Uttar Pradesh illiterate Dalitbahujan masses who preferred the Bahujan Samaj party and the Samajwadi party shows the direction of the future.

The Dalitbahujan movements, therefore, should be aware of the hurdles and complications that modern brahminical intellectuals— those who are abroad and those who are within India—are going to create. The hue and cry that they are going to raise against Dalitization among international circles will be great. We should aim for a cultural revolution that will avoid the loss of life. Dalitization must be handled very skilfully. All the theories that brahminical intellectuals have created in the name of nationalism, modernity, secularism and democracy bear the diabolical seal of Brahminism and Hinduism. The Dalitbahujan movements have not produced enough organic intellectuals to reinterpret the whole literature that emerged during the nationalist period and the post-colonial period. In order to dalitize society and de-Hinduize it thoroughly, every word and every sentence that has been written by brahminical thinkers, writers, politicians, historians, poets and art critics—virtually everything in every field—must be reexamined thoroughly. The task, however, is not going to be easy. To some extent, capturing political power is easy. But the Dalitization process is much more difficult, and if the Dalitization of society is not taken as a serious task, the question of sustenance of political power will not be possible. If the defeat of Shambhuka rajya or Ravana rajya are ancient examples, the drifting of the Dravida Munnetra political power into the hands of a Brahmin woman in Tamil Nadu is a recent example. It may not be long before the same state is recaptured by Brahmin men themselves.

The only way to historicize the past and safeguard the future is to create an army of organic intellectuals—men and women—from Dalitbahujan forces. Dalitbahujan organic intellectuals must work out a long-term strategy, both political and economic, to restructure social relations in a massive way. If the intellectual domain is as tortured today as the socio-political domain, it is because brahminical forces refuse to recognize the new ideas of Dalitbahujan organic intellectuals. Everything is shown in reverse order. If we say one thing, they understand it only in ways that suit them. When we did not ask them any questions they preached the 'correct' theories to us. Now that we are raising questions, they raise counter-questions. They doubt our intentions or integrity and our ability to sustain the battle. They suspect us in every respect. When we point out that they may be wrong, suspicion becomes their ideology. Now it is our turn to declare that suspecting them is a prime tenet of our ideology. Then they will stop asking questions. If they come at us from one end, we should begin from the other end. If the Brahminwaada represents the ideal for them, the Dalitwaada should be the ideal for us. Just as they are shouting from their rooftops (and they have very big houses) 'Hinduize India', we must shout from our toddy palms, from the fields, from treetops and from Dalitbahujan waadas, 'Dalitize India'. We must shout 'we hate Hinduism, we hate Brahminism, we love our culture and more than anything, we love ourselves'.

It is through loving ourselves and taking pride in our culture that we can live a better life the future.

AFTERWORD

On Being an Un-Hindu Indian

The main body of this Afterword was presented at a seminar at Columbia University, New York, in September 2002. A Rashtriya Swayam Sevak Sangh (RSS) woman activist, who lived in New York, protested and created a ruckus as she thought that the paper defamed Hinduism in a foreign land, that too in America, which is the other homeland of the Indian rich. Many of the Indian rich hate India as they think that it is a country that is not worth living in. Quite interestingly, there were many Indian settlers, who supported my broad arguments. The paper raised quite a lot of discussion and I thought it should become part of *Why I Am Not a Hindu: A Sudra Critique of Hindutva Philosophy, Culture and Political Economy* in the second edition and when it would be translated into another language.

In the course of its nine years of existence and circulation, many reviews of this book have appeared. Some of the reviewers pointed out some minor inaccuracies and flawed arguments, which are genuine in nature. At this stage, however, I am not making any changes in the contents of the book. Ever since it was published, the book achieved some victories, and it has also been subjected to some severe criticisms. It was the non-fictional bestseller of 1996. In the context of the world and the nation entering the new millennium in 2000, one of the very popular Delhi-based newspapers—*The Pioneer*—declared it as one of the five millennium books in the Dalitbahujan stream of writings. The most gratifying thing for me was that it was listed as a millennium book along with

Dr. B. R Ambedkar's *Annihilation of Caste*. Moreover, it has been translated into several Indian languages. In a way it has become a weapon in the hands of Dalitbahujan activists at a time when the Hindutva forces (the BJP and the National Democratic Alliance) were ruling the country.

Meanwhile, because of this book I got some visibility and some amount of space to write popular ideological articles in many mainstream newspapers in India. I travelled outside India to understand the socio-spiritual and economic alternatives for Indians. During this period, I wrote two books that Samya also published: *God as Political Philosopher: Buddha's Challenge to Brahminism* and *Buffalo Nationalism: A Critique of Spiritual Fascism*. Both these books show that my critic of Hinduism in the modern period has its roots in the Buddhist struggle against it in the ancient period, and that I am not criticizing Hinduism for the sake of criticism but presenting an alternative to Hindu spiritual fascism. During my journey of writing I have travelled from the stage of proposing Dalitization, as an idealist alternative in *Why I Am Not a* Hindu, to a concrete proposal of building Buffalo Nationalism as against Cow Nationalism of the Hindu brahminic forces. This Afterword gives a glimpse of the ideological and physical agony that I have undergone in writing such a book and also the gains I have attained by choosing writing as a process of thought reform.

Since India is a nation of plural cultures and is undergoing a socio-cultural revolution, several ongoing struggles of the Dalitbahujan forces and of the women's movement made my task rather easy. Of course, I had to face many attacks and insinuations in the process of my campaign for thought reform in India. The attacks of the brahminic enemies and the praise of well-meaning friends and critics neither unnerved me nor did they make me a self-satisfied being. I am one of those who believe in the famous saying: 'A dissatisfied pig is better than a satisfied man.' Particularly the attacks—of course not on my body but on my mind— emboldened me to continue my work further and further. For those who have been denied the right to write a text, writing a text of their own history and that of the Other is also a process of their socio-political movement. Though the movement of writing has its own limitations, it breaks the shackles of those who were denied writing. Writing becomes a weapon of the weak. In a casteist society, the brahminic forces who prevented this writing by the Dalitbahujans had made the physical struggles of millions of Dalitbahujans invisible. When a historical struggle becomes invisible, it does not kindle the fire of liberation. The process of writing in the face of bitter opposition is a torturous course. Yet this process has to go on without end. Let me, however, turn to the torment of being an un-Hindu Indian.

THE TORMENTS

It is more than a decade that the Mandal movement and the destruction of Babri Masjid took place. *Why I Am Not a Hindu* was written in the context of these two major events. It was aimed at contesting the concept of Hindu majoritarianism. I was the first Backward Class (OBC) person to deny the Hindu roots for Sudras as a whole, as indicated by the very title of the book. Though Mahatma Phule and Periyar critiqued Hinduism from the Sudra point of view, there is no literary evidence to show that they had disassociated the Sudra being from Hinduism from his/her very birth. Having come from a more suppressed untouchable background, Ambedkar said that though he was 'born a Hindu' he would not die as Hindu. Ambedkar accepted the brahminic definition of Hinduism and formed a critique based on its textual construction of caste and Hinduism. He evaluated these two institutions based on the Hindu scriptures. I took a different route to examine the fascist nature of Hinduism. In the day-to-day life processes of the Dalitbahujan masses much more concrete evidence of 'unHinduness' could be seen. In *Why I Am Not Hindu* I have examined Hinduism both as a way of life and as a religion to show how the Dalitbahujans have hardly anything to share with the Brahmin, Baniya and Kshatriya forces. In ritual practices and in all modes of cultures that govern human life the differences between the Dalitbahujans and the brahminic forces are too many and too visible.

As of now, I am an un-Hindu Indian. The brahminic forces hate my Sudra self-being that is conscious about being a Sudra. They know that that kind of consciousness has the historical ability of dismantling Hinduism itself. A section of the Dalit intelligentsia sees my position with scepticism and another section would see the historical possibility of forging a strong Dalit-OBC unity. Among the OBCs and Sudras (whom I have characterized as neo-Kshatriyas in my book) there is hardly any intelligentsia that is capable of involving itself in the philosophical discourses of caste and religion These people neither own the book nor do they totally disown it. Among them, those who are educated are focused on power and money, and many do not know what this debate is about. Yet in this situation they get neither power nor a share in the monopoly capital. They have blunted minds with a heavy superimposition of brahminic ideology. In my view, unless the battle is won in the spiritual realm as well as in the day-to-day life processes, they cannot succeed. A blunted mind does not perceive this fact or the truth hidden within it. As E. H. Carr said in his famous book *What is History?* A historical fact is like a sack and we need to fill it with philosophy. All the sacks of Indian knowledge must be filled with the Dalitbahujan productive philosophy. In a country where anti-productive Brahminism had established its hegemony, a campaign about productive philosophy and socio-spiritual equality is a tortuous course.

For taking up a campaign against Hindu spiritual fascism, I get a lot of hate mail and wild threats from the Hindutva and brahminical forces. In response to my articles on spiritual fascism and its implications for Dalitbahujan masses in popular newspapers, they wrote many abusive letters in the Indian media. Particularly after I wrote an article on the Gujarat carnage, 'Ayodhya: What Stakes Do OBCs Have?' (*The Hindu*, 18 March 2002), a threatening letter was addressed to *The Hindu* office, which was redirected to me. The un-named author of this letter, apart from abusing in filthy language, said, 'You are thinking of getting away from writing every nonsense—if you persist—please note that your head alone will he visible in the corridors of Salar Jung Museum' of Hyderabad. The Hindutva camp and the Brahmin Baniya organizations continue to write public and private letters attacking my mode of thinking and writing, which deconstructs their spiritual fascist being. They keep writing, which deconstructs their spiritual fascist being. They keep on writing to Osmania University, where I teach, demanding my removal from the university. I wrote in the introduction of *Buffalo Nationalism* how one of the Vice-Chancellors of Osmania University, Professor D. C. Reddy, through his Registrar asked me to stop writing. I am never afraid of these threats. At each stage I have become more determined to write more and more. When such attacks or threats were advanced, many Dalitbahujan youth and fellow activists firmly stood by me.

Brahminism has built a whole range of spiritually fascist structures in such a manner that it cannot extricate itself from those structures. What the Hindutva brahminic forces are afraid of is that the Dalits have a definite agenda of their spiritual liberation (most of them are embracing either Christianity or Buddhism), and if the OBCs, too, who are the main source of their muscle power, work out a spiritual liberation agenda, Brahminism and Hinduism will collapse like a house of cards. Their fears that their hegemony will be overthrown through the process of writing texts are very real because these expose their historical misdeeds. Their acts of desperation are getting more and more pronounced. Brahminism lives in a fear of the philosophy of equality, which germinated in their writing of Vedic texts with a theory of divine inequality. They constructed their God in their own image. Hence that God's body becomes the source of the caste system. That God begins to operate with weapons on his body. Using weapons to kill the lower castes becomes his divine essence. The very essence of the Hindu brahminic God goes against the philosophical tenets of the universal God. The universal God is benevolent. The hard working masses irrespective of colour, caste, creed and gender would be able to relate to this God and take him as theirs. God is not a killer. He is a reformer of individuals, social groups, nations, irrespective of their crimes, behaviour and attitudes. The Hindu Gods stood against all these benevolent attributes of God. This very fact of constructing an image of an inhuman God has done enormous damage to the nation. Of course such a God is constructed out of the image of the brahminic being. Such a construction was necessary for the sustenance and unproductive survival of the Brahmins.

In this book I have shown that there is a philosophical difference between the notion of God among the Dalitbahujan communities and the brahminic communities. Among the Dalitbahujan communities, God is an integrated self in their being, though God is not abstractly constructed as he is in universally expanded religions like Christianity and Islam. Both Jesus and Mohammed lifted superstitious societies out of their historical morass. But the Dalitbahujan masses of India remained at the level of idolatry with all positive signs of advanced societies in the spiritual realm. There is a need to search for Dalitbahujan God whose essence is humane—a God who loves human beings but never hates them. *Why I Am Not a Hindu* was written in the process of that search. A search for spiritual equality is not merely a spiritual act but a political act too. The relationship between spiritual and political agencies has been close and interwoven. This relationship gets extended to all spheres of life.

My writings in general and *Why I Am Not a Hindu* in particular addresses the Sudra/OBC constituency in its own language and idiom. The brahminic forces have no way but to engage with my writings because I am contesting the essence of brahminic culture and civilization and history. What I am writing today is the history of buffaloes whereas all schools of Brahminism have been writing only the history of cows in this country; cows that give hardly any milk. If some said the cow was/is a holy animal, others contested it and said no, it was/is a secular animal. Yet some others say no. . . no. . . cow is a social animal. But none talked about the buffalo. And ironically all of them involved in this destructive discourse have had coffee, tea, curd or buttermilk made out of only buffalo milk. The challenge before me and other Dalitbahujan intellectuals is to put the buffalo in the centrality of the discourse. I am as un-Hindu as the buffalo is, and I am as Indian as the buffalo is. Is not the 'Indianness' of the cow doubtful in an historical sense? Is not the patriotism of the brahminic forces really, really doubtful?

SPIRITUAL FASCISM

Hinduism is one of the four major religions of the world. Of these, Hinduism is the religion that commands comparatively the smallest number of people. It also commands the least amount of geographical area. Though all the brahminic writers claim that it is the oldest religion, the kind of Hinduism we are talking about, in the sense of religion, is of recent origin. The first ever usage of the word 'Hindu' in the sense of religion seems to have been done by Al-Beruni. The title of his book, *Al Hind,* seems to have been the first mode of construction in the beginning of the notion of Hinduism. The word 'Hind' but not 'Hindu' was used to denominate the non-Muslims of India by Al-Beruni. This seems to be the earliest form of construction of Hinduism as a religion—that too by a Muslim scholar. Here the word 'kind' seems to have been used in the sense of religion. Many Muslim scholars initiated the discourse around the non-Muslim population of India in geographical terms and called the people of that space Hind. The land in which they lived was called Hindustan. Of course, the nomenclature 'Hindustan' was used in the sense of 'Sindhustan', meaning thereby the land that surrounds the Sindhu River. Al-Beruni's usage of the word 'Hind' is exactly like the word 'Sindh'.

During the colonial period the Western Orientalists constructed all the non-Muslims as Hindus in the mode that they would construct Christians. In Christianity the right to read the book was granted to all. Untouchability or the concept of a human being as an untouchable is not known to them. They know racial segregation that was based on visible differences of skin colour. Western thinkers borrowed their language from the writings of Muslim scholars like Al-Beruni. Hegel in his major work, *Philosophy of History,* having compared the civilizational process of different nations, constructs Indian civilization as a civilization that did not form its own Spirit and did not have a History of its own. That is because 'everything—sun, moon, stars, the Ganges, the Indus, the beasts, flowers—everything is God to it'. Very surprisingly, Hegel knows that it was because of the caste system that it did not develop its soul. Though we are not sure whether he knew that there was untouchability in India, he treats all castes as Hindu. He, therefore, says, 'Each Hindoo assumes one definite occupation.' Hinduism did not become a religion like Buddhism, Christianity and Islam by evolving a universal soul of its own and could not allow India to become an historical nation because it built a spiritual fascist structure at the base of civil society. Whereas the other three religions built a spiritual democratic structure at the base of civil society, hence their soul and self acquired a definite historicity. Hinduism distributed socioeconomic and political power among the Brahmins, Baniyas and Kshatriyas. The 'feet-born' Sudra/OBCs have been relegated into a philosophical oblivion.

The Orientalists, without understanding its essence, projected Hinduism as a positive civil religion and the Brahmin nationalists used that Hindu religious identity as the other name of sanatan dharma in opposition to Islam and Christianity, as if spiritual fascism and spiritual democracies are comparable and contestable. There are practical inequalities in both Islam and Christianity. Women, particularly, suffer inequality in many respects in both Christianity and Islam. The ongoing debate, for instance, about Islam and the problems of burkha and talak are well known. However, in a fundamental area of spiritual area of spiritual equality at the level of book reading and the spiritual congregation, these religions had granted rights to women at an early period. The main difference between other religions and Hinduism is that the latter has an inborn spiritual fascist character. Religions like Buddhism, Christianity and Islam, on the other hand, as just mentioned, have the basic character of spiritual democracy. They have violated that basic 'essence and got involved in intra-religious wars. These wars sometimes are very brutal too. It is not correct to say that democracies do not fight with each other. There were historical phases in which religious wars and crusades took place. These religions were basically spiritual democracies. They were not political democracies. Spiritual democracy in itself does not resolve all socio-political problems. But it lays the foundation for socio-political equality. Religious democracy has its own historical contribution towards the overall growth of democracy as a system.

No religion except Hinduism built a structure of spiritual fascism to torture members of its civil society who are recognized to be part of that very religion. The Hindu religion has either to reformulate itself or Indian society as a whole should embrace religions that can deconstruct the spiritual fascistic social structures and establish spiritual democratic structures. *Why I Am Not a Hindu* was written with this objective in mind. During the six and half years f BJP rule they did not initiate any measures to reform Hinduism. Though the BJP talks about Hindu homogeneity, it made no attempt to decasteize Hindu society. On the contrary, it encouraged Brahminism to dominate and take control. The earlier reforms like the Bhakti movement only asked for Brahminization of Sudras by asking for spiritual rights. But that too did not change the caste system. I have no hope that the Hindutva school that essentially represents Brahminism could reform itself in future because both its day-to-day practice of Hinduism and its textual construction do not give any scope for reform. Even when the Hindu right wing as the BJP and the NDA were in power recently, they had not shown any indications of transformation. Now that they have gone out of power since the General Elections of 2004, they once again proved the point that I have made repeatedly in this book: that Hinduism is a religion of violence and a hardcore Hindu justifies violence as natural, as they did in the case of Gujarat carnage. From 'good' Vajpayee or intellectual Arun Shourie to so-called bad Narendra Modi to Togadia, all justify violence as desirable. If the violence is justified against the Muslims now, it was spiritually justified against the Dalitbahujans historically. Violence has been their creed. They love it and live with it. It was born and had grown with their spiritual fascist essence.

FIGHTING INTELLECTUAL UTOUCHABILITY

This book, as mentioned earlier, has been in the market for about nine years now. When I wrote the book I thought the Indian media would kill it either by total silence or by attacking it by all possible means. Writing an introduction to Jean Paul Sartre's *Being and Nothingness*, his English translator, Hazel E. Barnes, said, 'Any new theory [she actually quotes William James] first is attacked as absurd, then it is admitted to be true, but obvious and insignificant; finally it is seen to be so important that its adversaries claim that they themselves discovered it.' The Hindu tradition is such that the brahminic writers do not make claims for knowledge. In ancient times they declared that they themselves were 'knowledge' and the others were not even allowed to enter the discourse. In India, the discourse has been taken to a dead end. The written word has been made to be a living lie. In many countries the world over a written form was seen as the other form of truth. But in India Brahminism made it out to be the opposite. As a result, among the Dalitbahujans many proverbs came into being which make a mockery of the written word.

Given the predominance of the brahminical Hindu mind in the Indian press and English-educated upper caste social forces. I thought that my book would also be dismissed as 'absurd'. In a country like India where for thousands of years the creative genius of the productive Dalitbahujan mind was never discovered by its adversaries (the brahminical forces of all schools), the question of my book getting discovered by them even after my death would not arise. To recognize the strength of the adversaries the person or the social force in question should have the moral strength and an open mind trained in the civil societal structures, which nurtured that individual or that civil societal force. The training of the cultural process starts within the domain of spiritual culture of that particular civil society. A mind that is trained in the domain of the spiritual fascist culture like that of Hindu culture never appreciates the discoveries of its adversaries. Not that the adversaries of other religions are not hegemonic. Sometimes they are hegemonic and brutal. But the social cohesion in their societies becomes their strength. They might be exploiting other nations, but within themselves they keep struggling for socio-economic equality. Christian societies thus allowed socialist thought to emerge. Their capitalism has given rise to democratic egalitarianism. At the core of all this is the spiritual democratic structures that they established over a period of time. In India those who attempted serious social reform were never respected.

History had witnessed the fate of Phule, Periyar and Ambedkar. Phule in spite of being a great social reformer as kept under the carpet of history for several decades. Ambedkar, in spite of having the best mind, the best possible training to write in English, was certainly not discovered by the brahminical forces of India, even after forty-five years of his death. I, therefore, knew that the question of their discovering my book even after my death did not arise. There is a fundamental difference between the West and India. In the West the adversary of a writer reads any book written by anybody, including a book written by one's own enemy. The brahminic Hindus treat even the books written by Dalitbahujans as untouchable. Historically, not only the Dalit body but also books written by Dalit and OBC scholars remained untouchable. That was the reason why untouchability has been imposed on Ambedkar's theoretical writings for a long time in India. Intellectual untouchability was/is more dangerous than physical untouchability. The Dalitbahujan life has not been allowed to figure in school text-books. Their writings were not rejected with a critical assessment but were rejected with mere contempt even before reading. In such a situation there would not be any scope for discovering the contents of a book written by any person coming from such a social force. Though they are the producers of the historical ideas, producers of the wealth and the very structures of human survival, their ideas were seen as historically irrelevant. In a way, *Why I Am Not a Hindu* changed the environment of intellectual untouchability. It made its inroads into many brahminic houses. Perhaps this was the first book that many brahmin intellectuals read which contests their socio-cultural and economic being. This does not mean they recognize the worth of a book that their adversaries—the Dalitbahujans—write. But making them read the letter of the truth is a challenge before Indian history.

The basic question, however, is whom did I write the book for? Should any Dalitbahujan really look for the recognition of the Other? Or should we create our own readership, our own intellectual discourses where the brahminic texts get marginalized? Educating our own communities is more important than educating the exploiters in the struggle of socio-spiritual and economic liberation. More than the English book, the regional language translations are making a major impact on the mind of the OBCs and the Sudras as a large number of them are outside the pale of English-medium education. That is why I wished to have it translated into Hindi,[1] the language that many of the followers of Hindutva read. Among the Dalitbahujan communities, a book is not seen as an instrument of social transformation or liberation of an oppressed people. Their sense of liberation is very weak. The notion of spiritual and cultural liberation is a distant goal for them. Their socio-spiritual life revolves around the localized deities that I described in this book.

Though the worshipping of the local deity was positive in nature, the spiritual culture of the Dalitbahujans did not take them into the intellectual discourse towards the notion of an abstract God and the cultural and social economies built around it. Civilizations and cultures evolved only when the book and God became mutually relatable. Oral worship kept the communities linguistical illiterates as well. Because literacy and education have been slowly increasing among the Dalitbahujans and as a consequence there is an emergence of organic intellectuals—a source of fear among the so-called upper castes—a gradual change in the intellectual environment has begun to take place. There is some sort of intellectual negotiation between Dalitbahujans and upper caste women taking place. But the tension remains, which became very clear when the Thirteenth Trienniale of the Association of Commonwealth Literature and Language Studies Conference was held in Hyderabad in the first week of August 2004, under the leadership of a woman scholar, and not a single Dalit scholar/writer was invited to speak in any plenary session or to present a paper to represent her/his point of view of literary theory. Brahminism is an ideological construct that has gone deep into the psyche of brahminic men and women. Even a hundred Ambedkars would not be able to change their mindset because their minds are closed and locked up with a cultural key. It takes a long battle to change that very key itself. But such a situation does not make me hopeless. A shepherd relieves his long drawn out drudgery when his sheep delivers a lamb. I have enough hope on the lambs that are growing to maturity.

My early assessment of the context in which the book was written, however, was not entirely right. As I mentioned earlier, I wrote this book in the backdrop of the Mandal Commission, more particularly in the context of the destruction of the Babri Masjid, wherein the Hindu brahminical forces were on the defensive. This context was also mediated with the new social movements and thought processes of Dalitist, feminist, postmodernist and environmentalist ideological forces. In this process because of the feminist movement a small number, but a very influential one, of women—media people of an upper caste background—began to see the linkages between caste discourses and feminist discourses. The publisher of this book and those women who reviewed it come from that background. Subsequently those who supported me in the popular press, Malini Parthasarathy of *The Hindu,* Jayanthi of the *Deccan Chronicle,* Sagarika Ghose, a reputed journalist, Gita Ramaswamy, a Telugu publisher, and so on, subscribe to the notion of the liberation of women. In this situation, there was no way in which the Hindu brahminical forces could push the book under the carpet however hard they tried. The best way to make the anti-caste literature influential is to create a social bloc of readers, critics and propagators among the social forces that are fighting for liberation. No enemy recognizes marginalized men/women unless you threaten the enemy's very existence in every sphere of life. You must change the reference point, reference book and the reference mode of life it self. The Dalitbahujan literary movement is reaching that stage now. In Andhra Pradesh, for example, both brahminic spiritual and social writings and communist political and ideological writings have ceased to be the terms of reference. Thus, the situation is slowly changing. We are now at a stage of recognizing our own writings. The time is not too far off when the brahminic and communist forces need to look for our acknowledgement of their writings. This process has already started in many parts of India.

THE REVIEWS

The first review of *Why I Am Not a Hindu,* though small, appeared in *The Telegraph* (a Calcutta based daily, 12 April 1996) and it was written by a postmodern scholar, who saw it as an exercise in postmodern theory. A well-known feminist thinker, Susie Tharu, did a full-length review that put the book on the global map, with a serious critique of its positive and negative aspects. Her scholarship in the field of feminist studies is universally acknowledged, and it was published in a most respected Journal, the *Economic and Political Weekly*. Susie compared the book with Frantz Fanon's *The Wretched of the Earth* and said, '*Why I Am Not a Hindu* has much in common with Fanon's classic'. She went on,

> The emphasis in this study-cum-manifesto also is on the invisibility, indeed the repression in the Indian imagination (since brahminical values and knowledges are also anti-Dalitbahujan), of the lives, the worlds, the knowledges, the skills, the values, the narratives, the philosophical systems, the religious beliefs and practices of the huge majority of the women and men of the country. The questions that emerge from the book address all the key areas of our communal life.

Susie's review not only set the tone but also put the book on the philosophical map of the world. In a way Susie's review has dis-armed many potential attackers (not critiques) from both right and left wing brahminical forces. As the review had appeared in the *Economic and Political Weekly,* which is the most respected journal in the country, it provided me with the comfort of confidence.

Another feminist sociologist, who disarmed such forces, was Sujata Patel with her review in *The Hindu* (20 Oct 1996). Sujata described the book as 'a slim, provocative and brilliant polemical text' and said. 'We have perhaps for the first time a radical exploration of Dalit secular indigenous tradition.' Both Susie and Sujata's reviews were supplemented with the review of Gail Omvedt, well-informed critic, American-born, who became a citizen of India and committed herself to the Dalitbahujan cause. While accepting that 'it is brilliantly argued and the latest book in the tradition of social revolutionaries to reject upper caste dominance at the ideological and cultural as well as economic level,' she went on to say, '*Why I Am Not a Hindu* fails on two counts in asserting too much autonomy . . . . for Dalitbahujan culture and production relations and in allowing the brahminic upper caste culture to claim for itself the term "Hindu".' (*The Hindu*, 8 July 1997). Gail seems to think that Dalitbahujans could own Hinduism and the Other could be driven out of that space. In my view it is rather impossible because the nexus between Hinduism and Brahminism has been historical and it has been built quite consciously in the nationalist period too.

A very interesting review was that of a young Brahmin reviewer, S. Anand. While reviewing the book in *Deccan Chronicle* he appears to have revolted against the brahminical order in which he was born. He agrees with me in all seriousness that Brahminism as an ideology is anti-production, anti-humanist. The Goddess and God images of Dalitbahujan masses contain in themselves productive values and humanist morals, whereas the Hindu God/Goddess images contain only war and sex morals, an issue that needs to be examined by all Brahmin scholars with all seriousness. *Why I Am Not a Hindu* initiated that discourse which however needs to be carried further. Anand's review gives me the hope that Brahminism was/is developing serious cracks. He subsequently became an active campaigner of the book and of Dalitbahujan thought.

Surprisingly enough, so far, no feminist scholar coming from a Brahmin family has made a critique of the book in writing, though a lot about its negative and positive aspects—they found it to be more negative than positive—are being discussed. The need for debating the inter-relationship between the Dalitbahujan movement and the feminist movement has been well recognized. The liberation of both Dalitbahujans and women is closely related to deconstructing the spiritual fascist structures in whichever form they exist. Though all religions are patriarchal, the kind of oppressive structures that the Hindu patriarchy established are basically different from that of other religious patriarchal structures. If Indian feminists do not interrogate Hinduism from this angle, the cleavage between brahminic feminism and Dalitbahujan feminism will increase in the near future. Though Dalitbahujan feminism has its historic advantage of a positive man-woman relationship, because the overwhelming majority is illiterate, as compared to upper caste women, they are at a historical disadvantage. This does not mean that there is no male chauvinist oppression among Dalitbahujan communities. The difference is that upper caste male chauvinism is sanctified by the Hindu spiritual texts. Therefore, upper caste women suffer from the historic disadvantage of being under brahminic patriarchy and, thus, *Why I Am Not a Hindu* can work as a mediator between Dalitbahujan struggles and feminist struggles.

Several attacks appeared in print, both by liberal democratic Brahmins and non-Brahmin writers. M. V. R. Shastry, the editor of *Andhra Bhoomi*, a popular Telugu daily, wrote a lengthy, rather abusive article, and it was serialized in his paper for several weeks. The review was entitled 'Ilaiah Leela' (miracle of Ilaiah). Later it appeared in a poor English translation in a RSS English language magazine. The same review was again edited and reformulated into relatively better English by a New York-based group called Bharatvani Team, who wrote an introduction to the article and put it on their web site. In its Introduction, the Bharatvani Team says:

> Kancha Ilaiah's book *Why I Am Not a Hindu* is a manifestation of this disturbing trend. Ever since the book was published, Ilaiah has become a celebrity for various Christian missionary, Islamist, Indian Marxist and other Hinduphobic groups. The title ostensibly seeks to place the book in the league of texts such as Ibn Warraq's *Why I Am Not a Muslim* (New York: Prometheus Books, 1995) or Bertrand Russell's *Why I Am Not a Christian*. Ilaiah's book however differs from the others in its undisguised hatred for the targeted community (Hindus), for its crudeness, a general lack of scholarship and academic rigor, in the abundance of cheap rhetoric, in its distortion of facts and finally, in the author's total lack of understanding of the religion it seeks to denigrate. Surprisingly, the book seems to be quite popular in some American and European Universities. On various Internet discussion lists, scholars such as Lise McKean, Linda Hess, Eliza Kent, etc., routinely recommend it as an *introduction* level reading material on Hinduism! While one can understand the inclusion of critical views (provided they are scholarly) in advanced classes on individual religions, the inclusion of this hate-filled and negative text in *introductory* courses on Hinduism and India by professors (often of Marxist extraction) at schools such as the Columbia University, New York, is simply baffling, and also disturbing. One never encounters the inclusion of Warraq's text in *elementary* courses on Islam, or of Russell's classic in an *introductory* course on Christianity. Even for advanced courses on Hinduism, these learned professors should be able to find something that is more academic, instead of relying on a hate-filled tract.

Thus while the international Hindutva forces took up a hate campaign against the book they had to acknowledge the influence and the reach of the book. Shastry tried to ridicule the Dalitbahujan Goddess/God culture, dismissing it as a culture that had branched off from Hindu culture. My name, Ilaiah, was treated as a name that is not worth pronouncing properly. The name Shastry is a South Indian Sanatan Brahmin name. Those Brahmins, who are pundits in the Sanskritic Hindu Shastras, are given the name Shastry, and they are the perpetuators of caste and the worst practitioners of casteism. They hate all those human beings who bear names like mine. When you get humiliated because of the names that your parents have given you, as a symbol of your culture, it is a most disgusting experience, and M. V. R. Shastry in his review does that repeatedly. A Telugu reader, who reads his original Telugu review, can perceive the racist and casteist arrogance that underwrites it.

The RSS subsequently published this review as a booklet, which it distributed in Andhra Pradesh in a big way. If the name Isaiah has spiritual respectability in the Christian world, as one of the earliest biblical prophets, my name 'Ilaiah' which is a similar sounding one (with a difference that 'I' is in the place of 's') has no respectability within Hindu culture. My name did not come from a Christian background. Among SC/OBCs of Telangana it is a traditional name that has come from a Dalitbahujan God called iloni Mallaiah. He is also known as Iloni Mallanna. Iloni Mallanna was the God of sheep, goat and cattle. My parents after giving me that name had offered my first piece of cut hair to him. The Brahmin pundits in India think that our tradition, our Gods/Goddesses, our names have no cultural value and our culture has no historical value. They are upset because a person with this 'uncultured name' is writing history and arguing that 'our culture is also historical culture'. When the RSS entitled its abusive booklet as 'Ilaiah Leela' a Dalit journalist got upset and wanted to know how I would respond. My reply was simple. 'If their Gods like Brahma and Rama can play Leelas my Goddess Pochamma too can play her own Leelas. Our Goddess Pochamma has more Leelas than their God Rama has.' Having observed the intellectual tradition of the Sangh Parivar, one can safely say that they produced more abusers than analysts. They have no sense of productive culture and productive civilization. They think that the entire Indian civilization emerged from ancient Hindu books. They can never understand that all civilizations and cultures emerged out of human productive knowledge.

Of all the critical reviews, D. R. Nagaraj's review (*The Book Review*, October 1996) merits an examination. The very title of his review, 'The Pathology of Sickle Swallowing', shows that he was in serious disagreement with my propositions. His critique is based on his own knowledge of Kannada Sudra and brahminic cultures. He opposes the very methodology that I adopted to write this book and points out that Dalitbahujan and brahminic cultures are not as inimical to each other as I had shown in my book. Nagaraj seems to think that the negotiability between brahminic life, spirituality and culture and that of the Dalitbahujan was in-built historically. If that is so why is it that the culture of shoe making, pot making, sheep breeding and tilling the soil, which is integral to Dalitbahujan culture, did not become integral to Brahmin culture? Why did sickles and hammers become untouchable to Brahmin culture and to their Gods? Did Buddhism, Christianity and Islam de-spiritualize sickles and hammers? Nagaraj did not seem to realize that Dalitbahujans having operated with sickles and hammers had to swallow sickles and digest them too. Otherwise the nation would not have been what it is. The life of the Dalitbahujans who produced the wealth of the nation without even having any basic rights—the right to religion, the right to education and the right to equality—was a life of sickle swallowing. They must transform those sickles into effective instruments of writing.

Nagaraj seems to oppose the process of locating binary historical existences of Dalitbahujan and brahminical forces. The Dalilbahujans are now trying to retrieve the destroyed selves of their own in order to gain spaces that were not available to them all these years. When the Indian nationalist scholars are willing to analyse class and race questions in binaries why are they not willing to extend that method to caste? This is where I have a major methodological problem with secularist scholarship. Nagaraj, however, says, 'I am in total agreement with the larger political project of Kancha Ilaiah.' But what he does not agree with is my mode of positioning Dalitism to counter Brahminism. Dalitism and Brahminism have been contesting, each other throughout Indian history. The only difference is that Dalitist history remained in oratures whereas brahminic history got into literatures. Though both of them are histories, one in oral form and the other in literary form, the literary form is always presented as the truth. Dalitism is now transforming its oratures into literatures and in the process builds its own historiography.

Nagaraj does not seem to have realized that each political project has to evolve its own worldview. When a representative of the suppressed communities formulates his or her own worldview the oppressor naturally sees it as inimical. Why didn't Nagaraj, who was born an OBC, understand this simple dialectical process of existing binaries even in the caste system? This is where the caste-blind class consciousness of the Indian Left brahminized the Dalitbahujan intellectual. Nagaraj's arguments show that an otherwise brilliant intellectual like him got trapped in the ideological discourse of left Brahminism. This only goes to show that so long as caste and Brahminism are not dismantled, class ideology does not take a creative shape in India. Unless class formation takes a clear form, class ideology also will not form on proper methodological foundations.

Nagaraj seemed to have searched for soft options for repositioning caste relations within Hinduism and making it a religion in the sense that Christianity and Islam are. But by the end of his life (unfortunately he died five years back) he did not realize that such a soft option does not transform spiritual fascism into spiritual democracy. The Hindutva forces have proved recently that they could increase social tensions by strengthening the spiritual fascist tendencies in the Hindu caste system.

Those who are uncomfortable with the 'notions of binary opposition' would only end up in more and more confusion. The notion of what they call multi-dimensionality is capable of producing and reproducing Brahminism in each sphere, and there would not be any major opposition to its hegemony. The Dalitbahujan strength lies in locating the core of binary existences. Those Dalitbahujan scholars who let themselves be confused for three thousand years by falling into the trap of multi-dimensionality could never set a theoretical agenda of their own till Ambedkar came on the scene. He saw binaries through the prism of caste in Indian history as Marx saw the binaries in the West through the prism of class. Since *Why I Am Not a Hindu* comes from an OBC writer, the brahminical forces feel more threatened and raise all sorts of questions. The problem with an OBC intellectual like Nagaraj was that he had no theoretical identity of his own and he had no position on caste as a socio-political category. Caste in essence is a political category. Dealing with that institution from a politico-ideological point of view alone gives us scope to bring out the politico-ideological dimensions of the caste system. *Why I Am Not a Hindu* did that with some success. It put a manifesto of Dalitist ideology before the Indian nation. It evolved a course for Dalitization of the ideological discourses and also the socio-political structures. Though the book started as an autobiographical narrative, it builds a theoretical framework out of a social experience.

All major theoretical positions in the world emerged out of the author's urge for a search of identity, of a search for his/her history. A Dalitbahujan in India cannot search for his/her own identity in others' history. How can Dalitbahujans search for their historical identity in the Vedas, the *Ramayana*, the *Mahabharatha* and the Bhagavad Gita? Even assuming, as Gail says, that they should own Hinduism and disown Brahminism, even to do that the content and meaning of Hinduism would have to be changed. The socio-spiritual roots of the Indian nation should be reformulated and must be formulated in the image of Dalitbahujan productive culture, civilization and intellectual ethos. The concept 'Brahmin' in my diction does not mean knowledge. It means consumption of the socio-economic resources of the nation without investing any amount of labour power in it. It means consumption and destruction of national resources without any understanding and effort for rebuilding such resources. The concept 'Sudra' does not mean a particular people who are stupid with an un-cultured existence. It means the construction of the knowledge of production, of innovation of agrarian and artisan technology. The concept 'Chandala' does not mean unworthy of being a human being and leading an impure life in a spiritual sense. It means making the villages, the towns and the nation pollution free. The Chandalas are the builders of a culture that kept the living environment clean. It implies the transforming of skin into leather, into commodities. The notion 'Brahmin' in essence, on the other hand, represents unclean ugliness. The concept 'Dalitbahujan' now in essence means constructing the science of leather technology, building up the scientific use of manure, constructing the tools of production which not only improved our production but also kept our environment green and clean. Brahminism is the opposite of all this. It is the other name for consumption of natural resources without regenerating them. While Dalitism is positive, Brahminism is negative. India as a nation, thus, needs to undergo a revolution of reformulating knowledge and language.

Some scholars are worried that this discourse opens up a possible dichotomy between lower castes and communities in India, which they believe has not existed so far. There are serious fears about those who show the 'non-existing' dichotomy and then position it in a binary mode. They are of the opinion that such a discourse will lead to a civil strife. Some of these scholars, irrespective of their social or caste origins, are serious and well meaning. The fears of such binary positions come out very clearly in another review by Rajdeep Sardesai, a noted television journalist. In his review 'False Dichotomy' (*Biblio*, October 1996) he says, 'Unfortunately, Kancha Ilaiah himself got trapped in constructing a false dichotomy of an eternal conflict between the seemingly 'evil and oppressive' Brahmin-Baniya—neo-Kshatriya combine and the great and good Dalitbahujan Samaj, between an exclusionary Hindutva culture and an inclusive Dalitized India.'

The social forces that have made people live through a dichotomous social structure from childhood onwards prevent them from seeing the very existence of dichotomy. That is what conditioned consciousness means. As Karl Marx rightly located the malady, our social existence conditions our consciousness. In India caste as a social institution conditioned our consciousness more deeply than a civil society structured by class did in other countries. All Brahmin leaders and scholars during the nationalist period (Tilak to Nehru to Namboodiripad) never admitted that there was caste dichotomy in Indian society. For them such an admission was a self-destructive process because the very admission of such a dichotomy would have forced them to accept the exploitative hegemony that they established over the others. Opening up such dichotomous wounds would mean searching for remedies that reposition their socioeconomic existence. I do not think that a serious investigator like Rajdeep does not see the visible dichotomy between a Brahmin wada and a Dalit wada in the villages or between a Brahmin colony and a Dalit slum in Indian cities. But accepting that dichotomy in caste terms needs Dalitizing of one's own self. Dalitizing a Brahmin sell is not like proletarianizing a feudal self. In many countries, the later transformation became possible but the former transformation did not take place because of the very structure of the caste system. I am not saying that it is impossible.

And this has to happen only in India and so far it has not happened. So far no Brahmin born and brought up in this society has accepted the transformation into Dalitism. There is no record of this in the hitherto existing history. Hence there is no Brahmin scholar who could work out a solution to the caste question. All the attempts were only made by non-Brahmins. In ancient India, Buddha, a tribal prince, made an attempt but failed. In modern India Mahatma Gandhi tried to work towards abolition of untouchability (not caste) as he too came from a Baniya family. Even Ram Manohar Lohia tried to mediate between upper castes and lower castes to reduce the tensions in the caste hierarchy as he too was a Baniya. All of them failed quite miserably because Brahminism worked out ways and means to resist any reformatory agendas that came up from the dwija social forces. The abolition of caste requires a social revolution initiated and led by the organic forces that were victims of the very same caste system.

In a way a revolution was initiated by the organic intellectual forces starting with Mahatma Phule. That revolution was sought to be taken to a logical end by two great visionaries—Ambedkar and Periyar—who were born as Dalitbahujans in the context of the emergence of a nationalist brahminic social order. Ambedkar became an icon of the pan-Indian anti-caste revolution because he was the first untouchable in the whole of living Indian history who worked out a systematic theory of the annihilation of caste. Hence, after Buddha, Ambedkar acquired a prophetic stature in India. The three of them, however, denounced the caste dichotomy that was deliberately constructed by the brahminical order, as they were its victims. Their struggles in the historical background of Buddhism and also in the environment of existing spiritual democratic religions like Christianity and Islam are bearing some fruit.

It is for the victim to say whether dichotomy exists in a given society or not. Someone who has come from the social background of the victimizers—though his/her birth in that social layer is accidental—cannot sit on judgement of that social condition. The victim knows through his/her experience the pain of the dichotomy. After the formulation of theories of social justice by Buddha in India and several others who followed him (up to John Rawls), the victimizers lost the right to judge and the victimized gained that right to pronounce judgement from their position. Thus, being victimized itself is testimony enough for their righteousness. To learn how caste conditions consciousness in India, we need to see that the experience of people—the Dalitbahujans—is a testimony, which exists in an orature form. It now needs to be transformed into a literary form. No one born Brahmin, however great he/she is, will willingly allow this history to be written as the Dalitbahujans want to write it.

Gandhi and Lohia, who happened to be Baniyas, to some extent, admitted the dichotomous relations that caste created. All Brahmins, because they were Brahmin, were very silent on caste. Gandhi and Lohia had a contradiction and experience of caste suppression to the extent of the Baniya subordination in the caste system. Hence they talked against, at least, of untouchability. Phule, Ambedkar and Periyar because they were SC/BCs had to fight for annihilation or abolition of caste. Many Brahmin critics, of course, there are a few exceptions, even in this capitalist era, even though caste is very much alive in all spheres of life, believe that it does not exist: because they all do not want to see the existing dichotomy at all. Dichotomy in their view is a maya. But there is also a hidden conspiracy of silence in that existence. That silence works in favour of the hegemonic. If that dichotomy comes into the open, the fear of their historical hegemony getting overthrown becomes part of their existence. Every Brahmin intellectual knows that a caste war dislocates his or her power more than what a class war can do. In a class war, there is scope for manipulation whereas in a caste war there is none. In a caste society, class ideology can survive as a mirage. But when you actually approach that mirage of class it turns out to be caste. The discourse on caste dichotomy needs to take place to a much greater extent and unless one sees it in a binary form, as discussed earlier, the truth does not reveal itself. The truth formulates its identity only in contrast with falsehood. All identities are dichotomous binaries.

Rajdeep Sardesai attempts to establish a nexus between the Samajwadi Party and the Bahujan Samaj experiment and my theoretical discourse in *Why I Am Not a Hindu*. This, of course, is deliberate because he too knows all political praxis has its own course, which may not coincide with all dimensions of theory. The theoretical formulations about Dalitbahujan productive, rational and egalitarian living processes and their attempts to capture political power, though inter-linked, are two different processes. Secondly, Dalitbahujan morality and brahminical morality are two different worlds of morality. The Dalitbahujans are not bothered about the moral standards set by the brahminical forces as much as the brahminical forces were not bothered about the moral codes that Dalitbahujans set for society. The questions that I am concerned with in this book are about the very survival of Indian society. How Hinduism failed in constructing the dignity of labour; how it repeatedly attacked the productive values and energies of Dalitbahujan masses; and thereby how it attacked the productive culture itself. How it constructed violence as its social and spiritual essence. These questions are related to the issues that are beyond Kanshi Ram, Mayavati, Mulayam Singh, Laloo Prasad, and so on. Perhaps such questions could be seen, if at all one wants to see, in the light of what Buddha or Ambedkar practised, but not in the light of existing politicians' praxis.

While I am raising questions on the transformation of the whole of India, some of the critics pose contemporary political questions and attempt to frame my thesis in the narrow minded brahminical worldview. The question is that of teaching the new Dalitbahujan worldview to the brahminical forces of India. Many of my critics failed to understand that this is the larger dimension of my book. Any author who tries to demystify a historically mystified social system faces this huge backlash and that is understandable. But the most fundamental question that needs to be asked repeatedly is: how do we debate the issue of the abolition of caste? That is the reason why a serious engagement with commentators like Rajdeep should be kept going. Sadly, it is not possible to do so with people like Arun Shourie because of their negative attitude. Like their Hindu Gods they believe in the theory of 'an eye for an eye and a tooth for a tooth'. Dalitism stands on a higher pedestal and it works towards the marginalization of intellectual goondas like Arun Shourie and later to Dalitize them but not to kill them. Killing human beings is a part of *their* culture and reforming human beings is a part of *our* culture.

Another Brahmin reviewer (*The Indian Review of Books*) Trideep Surhud, a faculty member of the Dhirubhai Ambani Institute of Information Communications Technology, Ahmedabad, said,

> I am a typical representative of the caste/class group which has been instrumental in dehumanizing the vast majority of the Indians. I am aware of this. But this awareness by itself does not give any solace. Something about the book arises inner demons. Perhaps it is the undisguised, virulent criticism of Brahmin-Baniya culture, philosophy and political economy. Or perhaps it is the deep authenticity, anguish and anger of the author, the strong determination to overthrow this hegemony.

Further, with unusual humility for a Brahmin, he says, 'I find it impossible either to summarize, comment on or criticize the arguments presented in the book. Therefore, I wish to leave readers like me to discover their own sense of discomfort.' Trideep Surhud certainly is an uncommon Brahmin. The book has aimed at bringing forth such self-searching among the Brahmin-Baniyas, a first step in the process of Dalitization.

Dalitization, as I said earlier, is not an easy process. We need hundreds of Rajdeeps, Anands, Trideeps to continue to engage with Dalitbahujan discourse. But they must keep their eyes open. There are hundreds and thousands of Savarkars, Golwalkars, Vajpayees and Arun Shouries and, above all, dozens of Shankaracharyas in day-to-day touch with them because of their family and caste connections. They must have enlisted some Bangaru Laxmans or Uma Bhartis who are not as dangerous as the producers of Brahminism both in theory and practice on a day-to-day basis. They are Dalitbahujan beings ensnared in mental slavery.

One young feminist Brahmin woman of Delhi told me that a group of young Brahmin feminists read the book collectively. They felt terribly uncomfortable while reading the book as it revealed the unproductive parasitic nature of their own caste. They felt very disturbed. They discussed with their parents, who with the same discomfort that Trideep had encountered, told them that neither they nor their ancestors had been involved in productive work and experienced the pleasures and pains of that productive labour. She asked me, 'We have now realized that we were born and brought up in an unproductive parasitic culture, but what is the way out now?' A Brahmin woman's question should be taken as more truthful and genuine than that of a Brahmin man (of course this is also true of Dalitbahujans). Why? Because historically a Brahmin woman carries both geneological and experiential traits of Sudras or of modern Dalitbahujans than that of Brahmin men. I am not saying this out of imagination. There is huge evidence, in the authentic writings of Kautilya and Manu, that shows how Sudras and all women, including Brahmin women, were treated in the same demeaning way because they were seen to share the same genealogical origins. This could have been because most of the ancient Aryan invaders were men and they must have married the native Sudra-Dravid women. They must have had sex with such women and must have treated them as the equivalent to Sudra slaves. The male offspring begotten from those women must have been taken into Brahminism and the female offspring must have been treated as equal to their mothers.

Perhaps the authors of the earliest form of patriarchy, that too a brahminical patriarchy, could have been the Indian Brahmin men themselves. The dilemmas such Brahmin girls face appear to me to be genuine and serious.

I asked her, 'Did you not find a way out in the Dalitization chapter?' She said, 'Only to some extent.' The challenge before me or before any well-meaning Dalitbahujan thinker is to show an alternative that provides channels of transformation even for Brahmins, more particularly for Brahmin women. Some thinkers suggested that a serious solution to the caste system lies in liberating women from caste-based arranged marriages and providing a consciously constructed scope tor love marriages. But the historical indignity of labour and conditioned consciousness of food culture would become major hurdles for love marriages in India. Secondly, in the spiritual realm the so-called plural worship of war heroes and heroines (from Rama to Durga) in the name of Gods and Goddesses should be displaced with the worship of one philosophical notion of God/Goddess operating in the similar cultural realms, so that men and women coming from all castes share the same spiritual culture, food culture and work culture and so on. If a Rama worshipping vegetarian and a Pochamma worshipping meatarian, with different work cultural ethics, enter into a love marriage that marriage cannot last long because of the huge cultural differences.

We have to address these questions before we address the question of love marriage. I rather strongly feel that such an alternative does not get located in isolation. We must examine Indian society from the caste-point of view in greater detail. We have to make a long journey in this direction. It is a historical fact that no single writer can provide solutions for the myriad historical problems that a caste-centred society like ours engendered. Buddha tried to work out some alternative structures, which were dismantled by Brahminism over a period of time. Ambedkar made a major attempt to provide an alternative ideology; even that was not allowed to emerge as a full-fledged model. Brahminism is too powerful a system to be broken within a short time. And it needs a generational construction of alternative knowledge systems.

THE TRANSFORMATIVE PROCESS

Indian society is undergoing a transformation that earlier generations had never witnessed. This transformation mainly locates itself in demolishing caste structures. The brahminical forces were the main beneficiaries of the Indian caste system. As caste is crumbling down, the brahminical forces feel that the earth under their feet and the sky over their heads are also crumbling. It is with this feeling of loss of their selfhood, hegemony, moral and political authority that they are making attempts to attack the Dalitbahujan tradition. The recent attacks of the Hindutva theoreticians such as Arun Shourie show that they are becoming increasingly desperate. *Why I Am Not a Hindu* aims at destroying the very basis of brahminical hegemony. This is the latest and the most noticed text that was constructed as an expression of post-Independence Dalitbahujan consciousness. This consciousness has the most revolutionary potential than the one expressed by earlier generations and ages. The most advanced strength of the contemporary Dalitbahujan an consciousness lies in its post-Ambedkarite existence. Ambedkar wrote two extremely important texts that initiated a revolutionary process: *The Indian Constitution* and *The Annihilation of Caste*. Ambedkar laid a much broader and stronger foundation than all other anti-Hindu thinkers, more particularly than that of Periyar, Phule and Buddha.

The first major text that attacked the Hindu varnadharmic thought was the *Digha Nikaya*. This text emerged from the original discourses of Buddha, and it was said to have been compiled by Upali (a barbar by caste) after Buddha's death. The second major text was *Gulamgiri*, written by Mahatma Jyotirao Phule in the mid-nineteenth century. The most revolutionary text that followed Phule's text was *The Annihilation of Caste* written by Ambedkar in the mid-twentieth century. *Why I Am Not a Hindu*, as Gail Omvedt put it in her review, came in this tradition as a reflection of the aspirations of post-Ambedkarite Dalitbahujan thought. Hence it stands on the shoulders of Ambedkarite methodology and attempts to construct a synthesis of the ideological process that is at work.

Methodologically, as some critics have said, it is neither an autobiography nor a book on my caste. It is a text that aimed to play a critical role in the Dalitbahujan revolution. This fact was well understood by my serious critic, Dr. Nagaraj, who said, 'The radical passion of this book and the political agenda of the Dalitbahujan movement sustain each other.' He realized that it doesn't talk about one caste nor about many castes. It synthesizes the historical experience of all the Dalitbahujan castes. Of course, like many serious investigators and builders of ideas and thought from the toiling masses, I encountered many problems in writing this book. While formulating a methodology, presenting the material and constructing arguments in a communicable form, I had my own limitations. It was a new experiment. I was aware that all experiments are bound to face resistance from several forces in India. The Indian upper castes refused to conduct experiments. There is an increasing need for experimenting in the field of writing.

Both in written criticism and also in oral discourses many said that the alternative that *Why I Am Not a Hindu* constructs is not a full-fledged one. The last chapter 'Dalitization Not Hinduization' just opens the lock. It has been incorporated in a major anthology of postcolonial studies brought out by Routledge. I thank the editors for doing so. Frankly speaking, I myself was not clear about the socio-political and spiritual alternative that one can establish in such a brutally constructed unequal society. Though the whole blueprint of the Marxist alternative was there before me, I was of the opinion that it only helps us in methodological terms. We must construct an alternative, rather, search for one, within our own civil societal structures. The Buddhist Sama Sangha was a model that was available in the Indian context. It was an ancient experiment and not a very successful experiment at that. After some time Hinduism was able to destroy it. I, therefore, started looking around, searching for a model within my own reach. One way was to locate such an alternative in Indian tribal society. Marx seems to have located his 'primitive communism' within the tribal mode of economy and culture. L. H. Morgan located an alternative for positive woman-man and marriage relations again in a tribal mode (of course in American-Indian tribes), but I thought that the tribal model does not provide an alternative for a hierarchized caste system. An alternative model must be located amongst those who have been fighting against Hinduism for centuries. They must also have their roots non-tribal civil systems. I realized that the Dalit wadas—the Maadigaa wadas, the Maalaa wadas, the Chamar wadas—provide the best models of an alternative. A serious study of Dalit wadas in terms of their philosophy, culture and political economy will set us on a different course of thinking. The last chapter opens the lock of Dalit society in that direction.

It is more difficult to understand Dalitbahujan society than brahminical society. Brahminical society has been studied in detail over a period of centuries. One can read about it in the texts—from the Vedas to autobiographies of several Brahmin men and women. To understand Dalitbahujan society not much written material is available; only recently have some basic texts been constructed. The Hindu schools constructed texts that show Dalitbahujans only as uncivilized and historical people. This was the most destructive aspect of the Hindu mind, thought and ideology.

When I show an altogether different existence, different relations, more positive and scientific productivity of labour, all Hindu minds get shocked. They think that the writer who is constructing such socio-economic process within Dalit wadas must be mad. Even persons coming from brahminized OBC castes, who lived in their childhood in an environment of brahminic pooja, janzam (the so-called sacred thread) on the bodies of their men, think that this is mad man's work. Those few Dalitbahujans who get some money and marginal social status keep moving into the Hindutva fold. They too think that such discourse is harmful to their own interest and hence harmful to the nation itself. They too try to distance themselves from all these ideological discourses. It is easy to get a Dalitbahujan whose productive roots are just cut off or in the process of getting cut off to attack another Dalitbahujan. If one's mother had no interaction with agrarian work and one's father had no interaction with the productive process and looking after the living process of animals and birds, the family develops a hatred towards such a work. Children do not learn anything positive about such work in an educational environment wherein the dignity of labour has no place.

But a peripheral integration of a small section of Dalitbahujans into Hinduism as unequal partners does not transform the system that stood against the whole nation's advancement. A Hinduized mind acquires all the characteristics of understanding myth as reality and reality as myth. Such brahminized Dalitbahujan academics, who write, as Marx said, pedantic abstract mythical material, keep saying that Ilaiah sees caste everywhere. Caste is everywhere in India and the roots of caste are in the heart of Hinduism.

The Dalitbahujan movement of India faces a major problem in making Dalitbahujan scholars unlearn what they have learnt in brahminical educational institutions. In many universities Brahminism is coached in the jargon of Marxism and the forces that get trained in some institutions within India and abroad attempt to ignore texts like *Gulamgiri*, *The Annihilation of Caste*, and *Why I Am Not a Hindu*. In the process of engaging with the discourses of communalism and secularism, they made Savarkar's *Hindutva* or Golwalkar's *Bunch of Thoughts* more popular than any other positive texts constructed by Dalitbahujan scholars in opposition to the Hindutva texts. Can secularism be secularism while remaining silent about caste? Is not casteism an integral branch of communalism? As an un-Hindu Indian I would like to ask the scholars, including the NRI scholars and the scholars at home: are not Vajpayee and Advani modern avatars of Rama himself? How does Rama become a Hindu Maryada Purushothama and Advani become an Amaryada Purush when both of them practice violence as creed?

Rama killed Tataki, got his brother Laxmana to cut the nose and earlobes of Shurpanaka, as she was one of the most beautiful Dravidian woman, killed Bali, Shambuka and the entire Ravana dynasty. He had no hesitation to burn his wife alive—which would have happened if she had not walked out of the agnipareeksha or ordeal by fire alive. All this violence was against Dalitbahujans and women. He made his Dalitbahujan disciple Hanuman kill many and justify that violence in the name of protection of Hindu Ramarajya. Doesn't what happened in Gujarat under the supervision of an OBC disciple of Vajpayee and Advani—Narendra Modi—present the same pattern of violence? *Why I Am Not a Hindu* opposes both Rama's violence and the violence of Ramarajya. Is it not important to debate how Hinduism and Hindutva are two sides of the same coin called spiritual fascism? Can you love one and live in it and hate the other?

Hyderabad, March 2005

1. में हिन्दु क्यों नहीं: हिन्दुत्व दर्शन, संस्कृति और राजनीतिक अर्थशास्त्र का एक शुद्रवादी विश्लेषण (Feb 2006).

About the Author

Kancha Ilaiah Shepherd recently retired as Director, Centre for the Study of Social Exclusion and Inclusive Policy, Maulana Azad National Urdu University, Hyderabad. He is Chairman of Telangana Mass and Social Organizations (T-Mass) that works for English-medium education. He has helped to build up Dalit-Bahujan and civil liberties movements in India. He received the Mahatma Jyotirao Phule Award, 2000.

His paper 'Experience as Framework of Debate', which appeared in the *Economic and Political Weekly*, set up new terms for the debate on the reservation policy during the anti-Mandal struggle in 1990. His contributions have appeared in *Economic and Political Weekly, Frontier* and *Mainstream*, and in major national English dailies like *The Hindu, The Times of India, Hindustan Times, The Indian Express, Deccan Herald* and *Deccan Chronicle*. He is also a regular contributor to Telugu magazines and to dailies like *Vaartha and Andhra Jyothi*.

As his books raised a major debate in English and other regional media, he wrote a book in Telugu, *Manatatwam* (Our Philosophy), which put the Dalit-Bahujan productive philosophy in a new per-spective. The book became an ideological weapon among Dalit-Bahujan and Left circles in Andhra Pradesh. Among his books are *Turning the Pot, Tilling the Land: Dignity of Labour in Our Time* and *The Weapon of the Other: Dalit-Bahujan Writings and the Remaking of Indian Nationalist Thought*.

Kancha Ilaiah Shepherd was a post-doctoral fellow with Dalit Freedom Network, Denver, Colorado, 2004–2005, and as a member of the network, he has deposed before several international com-mittees about the historical role of caste and untouchability in sus-taining a modern form of slavery in India. He was a member of the National Campaign for Dalit Human Rights (NCDHR) that took the caste and untouchability issue to the UN Conference on Racism, Racial Discrimination and Xenophobia at Durban in 2001.